## Endorsements

"With the benefit of my nearly half a century of reading excursion, I can confidently endorse the author's narrative in Waves of Destiny as quite captivating, revealing and, purposeful. It is not commonplace for one individual to knit such a bold and intriguingly suspense-filled web of waves, so foamy and torrential; Waves of Destiny. Curious! Agitated!"
 Dr. Emmanuel Ojukwu, Commissioner of Police (retired)

***

"This is the only book in all my life that I have had to read with candlelight when electric power failed. I just could not drop it."
- Victor Anoliefo, Quill Master, Abuja Literary Society.

***

"A great literary piece! Sheer brazenness! Firm gripper! Unputdownable!"
- Coli Steiner, International Book Reviewer.

***

Other books by the author:

*Bow You Must*
*The Forest Dames*

# WAVES OF *Destiny*

ADA AGBASIMALO

Waves of Destiny by Ada Agbasimalo

ISBN 978-1-952027-84-0(Paperback)
ISBN 978-1-952027-85-7 (Hardback)

This book is written to provide information and motivation to readers. Its purpose is not to render any type of psychological, legal, or professional advice of any kind. The content is the sole opinion and expression of the author, and not necessarily that of the publisher.

Copyright © 2021 by Ada Agbasimalo

All rights reserved. No part of this book may be reproduced, transmitted, or distributed in any form by any means, including, but not limited to, recording, photocopying, or taking screenshots of parts of the book, without prior written permission from the author or the publisher. Brief quotations for noncommercial purposes, such as book reviews, permitted by Fair Use of the U.S. Copyright Law, are allowed without written permissions, as long as such quotations do not cause damage to the book's commercial value. For permissions, write to the publisher, whose address is stated below.

Printed in the United States of America.

New Leaf Media, LLC
175 S. 3rd Street, Suite 200
Columbus, OH 43215
www.thenewleafmedia.com

# Contents

Dedication ..................................................................vii
Acknowledgements......................................................ix
Foreword ....................................................................xi
Preface ......................................................................xiii
Prologue ....................................................................xv

Chapter 1:   Naminsa............................................................1
Chapter 2:   Oil in our land, fish in our water .............................5
Chapter 3:   The Expedition ................................................10
Chapter 4:   The Escape Bid ................................................13
Chapter 5:   Justice from Minja............................................18
Chapter 6:   The Raboni Home ..........................................23
Chapter 7:   The he-Goat..................................................29
Chapter 8:   The Fairy Tale ................................................32
Chapter 9:   The Striking Resemblance................................36
Chapter 10: The Good Samaritans .....................................39
Chapter 11: Everywhere I go I see you .................................47
Chapter 12: The Big Apology .............................................52
Chapter 13: The Big Surprise.............................................59
Chapter 14: The EDD........................................................66
Chapter 15: Let Go............................................................73

Chapter 16: Who? Who? Who? ..................................................78
Chapter 17: The Five Bs ..........................................................89
Chapter 18: Volumes ................................................................97
Chapter 19: Solace ..................................................................107
Chapter 20: Bad News Everywhere ......................................109
Chapter 21: Overfull Gutters .................................................112
Chapter 22: The Specialist .....................................................119
Chapter 23: The Twins were Girls.........................................125
Chapter 24: The Informants ..................................................136
Chapter 25: Crime does not pay ............................................142
Chapter 26: All Humans, God's Creation ............................145
Chapter 27: Crossing the T's and Dotting the I's ................152
Chapter 28: Well Done, My Girl ...........................................159
Chapter 29: Calm an Enraged Lion ......................................162
Chapter 30: Oh My God! .......................................................165

# DEDICATION

To the victims of all forms of violence and abuse, especially:

To the girl child

To the Oil Riverine Area

To humanity

# ACKNOWLEDGEMENTS

Firstly, God Almighty! Then to:

Engineer Emmanuel Obiora Agbasimalo and our quartet

Mum Dorothy Okere, moral energiser; and siblings, great encouragers

True friends, both older and younger

All earnestly appreciated

# FOREWORD

*Waves of Destiny* arrives with a fresh reading delight, years after the author's first book, *Bow You Must*, which dauntingly laid bare the hushed pains of a part of humanity, in most of the developing world.

The main focus of this new book remains the same issue, which the author is most passionate about – the psychosocial status of the feminine personality in any society driven by trado-cultural patriarchal trappings.

The author identifies uneasy thorny materials posing challenges, and makes an attempt at converting them into useful products, detailing a young girl to play a decisive role in the quest for definite solutions to religious and ethnic intolerance in Nigeria, which result in major conflicts and their attendant negative consequences. She also tries to weave the personality and destiny of a young woman into the Niger Delta and its issues of oil exploration, pollution in the creeks and the fishing waters and the economic disempowerment of the people who rely on fishing. Creating suspense upon suspense, the author ingeniously crafts these issues into a story in which a woman's ability to pass a thin thread through the issues is lauded. Knitting these issues into a web of a curious blend of ignorance and bravery, sacrifice, hate, anger and determination, kindness, joy, peace, regrets, victory and lessons; lessons learnt. Without overflogging any issue, the author constructively paints a non threatening picture of the travails, vulnerability and discrimination inherent in the mishandling of gender matters, and the negative consequences that trail them. Indeed the issues addressed in the book are all current priority concerns in the Nigerian society, and they all have the potential of impacting on sustainable development in the society at large. The author seems to have developed herself to a point where her works are looked out for, with interest. I indeed cannot wait to read Ada's follow up book where I am sure she will address more food-for-thought issues, in a fast-pace *unputdownable* way, like she has done here.

The book is recommended to everyone concerned about the development of peace and equity in any environment. Go pick a copy!

Dr. (Mrs.) Yerisoibiba Chidi

# PREFACE

It is incredible how waves of destiny toss people around. With body and mind working in consonance, the strong might attempt to withstand the force but it is not usually the same with the vulnerable and psychologically tortured.

The author, within the pages of an amazing work, paints a big picture of today's issues in a multi-ethnic, multi-cultural, multi-tribal, multi-talented, multi-populated and multi-plagued country. These issues designed to keep the reader focused on a multi-dimensional intrigue, also create space for the author to demonstrate that for some, the path is tortuous from the cradle to the grave.

'Waves of Destiny' is an exposition of a tradition of man's inhumanity to man, survival of the fittest, and thoughtlessness. It also showcases industry, kindness and love, peace and unity, consideration, motherhood, resilience and focus. What juxtaposition, you would say!

Ada Okere Agbasimalo Ph.D

# PROLOGUE

The rib and the womb!
From the rib some were formed.
In the womb all are re-formed
The rib, semi - straight
On a mission to mate
The womb, a receptive hollow
Semi-straight in hollow
Pain of our world
Root cause of gender odd:
Rape and indecency
Forced pregnancy
Perhaps abortion,
Bucks for conjugal action
Transmitted infection
Regrettable commotion
Like hell and its fire!
Oh! What a quagmire!
But alas! The tigress re-emerges!
Gathers the bits and pieces!
Mold! Mold! Mold!
Her giant strides, bold

She towers above the odds
Her reward tall as rods
Her name becomes aplomb
Despite the rib and the womb
Her survival mission never to cease
For victory means peace!
*Ada agbasimalo* PH.D

# CHAPTER ONE

# Naminsa

The landlocked community of Naminsa remained hostile to Oyiga Silas and Rita, his wife. The twosome had come a long way. Biase, their teenage daughter and only child, also got a taste of abrasive manners from the community's kids. Even the kids! The couple still had reasons to smile at intervals. This rural community where they hailed from could boast of a big market. Oriosha market attracted traders and buyers on a daily basis, recording a once-a-week high flow, when traders from far and near came in large numbers to buy and sell food items and other commodities.

On such market days, the untarred road leading to Naminsa witnessed a huge vehicular traffic and a massive inflow of people. As early as six in the morning, the rather sleepy community had started bustling with slim women with firm bodies carrying their wares on their heads and walking briskly to the marketplace, some with their babies firmly strapped to their backs and others with their older children trailing them with relatively heavy loads. Women with well protruded bellies were seen with loads on their heads, trudging to the market as if led by the foetus. Overloaded motorcycles making their runs combined their noises with those coming from loaded pickup vans, squeaking bicycles and crackling wheelbarrows. It was also time for the community to inhale different textures of vehicular fumes. It gave them a feel of city life. After all, they imagined, it happened the same way in big cities like Port Harcourt, Lagos and Onitsha.

Naminsans enjoyed this weekly quickening of their environment and seemed not to bother about the combination of fume and dust, causing them to cough and sniffle from time to time. It indicated to them that external wealth was filtering into the community and hard-working women got another opportunity to stuff the waist pouch with money, the smile in their hearts making little effort to show on their faces. Their hardworking men put no one in doubt that muscular power could be converted to cash. They lifted heavy objects to different stalls and displayed their goods for sale.

The haggling, exchange of cash, banters and greetings made a world of difference. That one day in a week, meals got more delicious; husbands lightened their frowns and softened their all-hard stance, and their wives lost their urge to complain. Many wished everyday was the weekly market day.

Danny parked his motorbike and rushed in for a bath. The day's sales were big and he bubbled with joy. His newly married wife, Virginia, had prepared dinner and an irresistible aroma filled the house. With his towel round his loins, Danny rubbed his palms together and licked his lower lip.

"Oh Virgie, please come. This food is already doing some things inexplicable to me."

"Ha! What could that be? You have not yet eaten the food."

"But the aroma is like an aphrodisiac."

"Hey Danny boy, eat the food first, then later…" Virgie winked at her smiling husband.

The weekly market day can have different effects on families, buyers and sellers.

"Wait a minute, you have scratched my leg with your…"

"Don't you hear well? Are you deaf? Didn't you hear the sound of the wheelbarrow when I was coming? Please give way, I am in a hurry."

Beriso did not know which hurt the most, the interruption, the rudeness or her scratched leg. The wheelbarrow boy tried to move away through the other side of the way, struggling with his overloaded mini truck but Beriso, who apparently had had enough grabbed the boy by his dirty shirt and shook him.

"Enough has to be enough. You did not only scratch my leg, your cranky truck tore my wrappa. I am not only going to take the anti-Tetanus Toxoid, I am also going to fix or replace my torn wrappa and you are not even remorseful. You must pay for everything, today and now." Still grabbing his shirt with one hand, she slapped him on the cheek and back with the other hand.

"Yes, deal with him. Last week, one of them hit an old woman and got her limping. Another scattered my wares and got me gathering the ones that were not smashed. Deal with the idiot. Should we run away from this market because of wheelbarrow boys?"

"Woman, please mind your business. You are not the one involved now," said the wheelbarrow boy, as he turned to the other woman who just complained.,

"Eh, he still has the mouth to talk," the woman howled, also hitting him, as she talked.

"Shut up, you scoundrel! You still have the guts to talk. Who is your mother? Can you talk to her in that manner? Did she feed you with breast milk or goat milk? Tell her I asked," another woman retorted, raising her hand to hit the lad, but refrained.

The boy glared at the three women.

"Hey, what is going on here?"

The women turned to see where the male voice came from, and just then, the boy forcefully thrust himself backward, freeing himself from the woman's clutch. He escaped into the crowd, abandoning his loaded wheelbarrow. The man's effort to catch the fleeing youth was futile. He had only come to the market with his friend to buy some good locally-made shoes.

"Hey Maa'ma, is it because of this small scratch that you want to kill the poor boy?" another wheelbarrow boy passing by scorned. News had quickly gone round that one of them was in trouble. Beriso and the others paid him no heed. It was usual for them to take sides with their member, whether at fault or not.

"What about the yams and grains? Who owns them? The barrow is overloaded," another man asked. The crowd had grown bigger. Suddenly, they saw a woman running towards the crowd.

"Ewuo, my goodness, I am so sorry about the trouble he has caused you. Everyone complains about the unruly behaviour of these boys. It is too much. The boy actually ran to me to tell me he got into trouble and managed to escape. That's why I hurried down. The items belong to me. I had asked him to bring them to my stall from a wholesaler. As I was wondering what kept him, I saw him running towards my stall, panting. You must have given him a scare and I am glad to see that they can be rattled, these wheelbarrow boys. I am indeed sorry about the scratch and your torn wrappa."

"Sorry, Madam," everybody echoed.

"That's okay," Beriso said, moving away slowly.

Oyiga and his wife had built their fish trade into a business that had customers queuing up to buy from them. Their smoked fish, oozing a nostalgic fish oil aroma from the smoke, attracted so many customers that they hardly had any leftovers. On the big market day, their stall always was a focus of sorts. Before mid-day, Oyiga and Rita had exhausted their stock, cleared up their shed and were ready to go home. Oyiga usually went home before his wife to count and recount the money made from the day's sales, in preparation for the next trip to the creeks to get more fish.

The handsome profit he recorded brought a grin to his face as he tucked away some of it. Rita stayed on a little longer to buy ingredients for her family's extra delicious meal of the day. Biase kept the home and read her books in their absence. On school days, she was busy with her studies while her parents nursed the business that took care of her school fees.

Naminsa was not a fishing community. Oyiga was about the only big fish seller in that community market and had to workhard to keep up the pace.

# CHAPTER TWO

# Oil in our land, fish in our water

Oyiga's peopele wished he took a second wife if only to give him more babies. Sixteen years after their first child, they had been unable to have another one. It was unusual in Naminsa for a childless couple or those with only one child not to do something urgently about it, especially if that only child was not endowed with the serum of procreation. It was also unusual that Rita appeared so unconcerned about their plight that she had not hastened the move to get her husband to father babies through another woman. Oyiga's forty-one years on mother earth coupled with Rita's thirty-six seemed to have bestowed on them a maturity that made their reasoning completely different from other community members. Biase just turned 16 and had grown into a pretty dark-skinned adolescent girl, under the close supervision of her parents. She made good grades, for which the community school was not exactly known.

The family's medium-scale fish-smoking industry yielded enough income to see their daughter through school and still save for the rainy day. Oyiga usually travelled to riverine communities to buy fish freshly caught by fishermen, who usually displayed their catch by the riverside. He brought home the fish and Rita smoked them with Biase's assistance, and put them on display for sale. He bought from several riverside fishermen and amassed them at one spot. After a long ride on a broad tarred road, the lorry got to a bye pass junction to Naminsa where Oyiga would hand over his sacks to waiting wheelbarrow boys who usually trudged for about ten minutes to get to Oyiga's grilling shed where they offloaded the sacks. The boys usually smiled back to the bye pass junction with empty barrows, eagerly awaiting the next opportunity. Whenever the stock of grilled fish reduced considerably, Oyiga found the need to return to the creeks for replenishment. One day he and other fish traders got to one of their favourite fishing communities and found all the fishermen sitting on overturned fishing boats, with hands on cheeks.

"Bros, wetin happen nah?" Oyiga asked

"Wetin happen? Na dem poison naim don kill all de fish. Look inside water meyu see as fish jus die finish," one of the sorrowing fishermen said.

The traders turned and looked into the river and were horrified at the sight of dead fish all floating, so many of them. Oyiga could not help imagining how much profit he would have made from the purchase of so much fish. This was not the first time the fishing community was being deprived of their source of livelihood. They depended a lot on fish as merchandise and for food, and whenever there was pollution from the oil rigs or from other sources of crude oil products, they suffered a great deal because of this harmful effect. Many foreign oil companies had made a haven of the environment where oil had been found and where oil rigs abound. They lived in opulence amidst several poor residents.

"This is callous! It is insensitive and without regard for aquatic life and human livelihood. It is an environmental sin," shouted some of their vocal elite kinsmen, in a fiery discussion with others.

"It is sure wicked and careless, and the government is not even doing anything about it," replied another.

"What government? Does the government know that you exist? Where is the proof? Just look around and show me the proof. Yet the black gold underneath only performs its wonder elsewhere while the goose that lays the golden egg remains shabby and without egg to eat," said one other man.

"Oh yes! Without egg to eat, the people become hungry and malnourished. You know, a hungry man is an angry man, who might someday get propelled by the anger to take laws into his hands. This is simply why there is so much restiveness around. My vision is that if government does not quickly nip it in the bud, it might get beyond control. It has been said that anyone pushed to the wall always finds a way of fighting back," yet another man said. But as serious as that comment was, Oyiga and his fellow traders were only concerned about was how to get their usual supply of fish.

"The oil is in our land, the fish in our waters. They use our oil to poison our fish and leave us destitute and hungry. Those white people look very healthy and live in wealth just next to our shanties, and pretend not to notice our plight. Maybe they have no conscience but I think that if they know what is good for them, they should plough back into our communities and also do something positive about this perennial pollution that deprives us of our much loved fish, otherwise, the restiveness will increase and might get beyond control. Do not say I did not tell you o."

"Pariso!" another community member called out to the last speaker.

"Why are you talking about the white men only? What about your fellow black countrymen who used political power to appropriate your oil portions from which they make a fortune? Do they give you and me any? What about their sons and daughters who have been made to take over the administration of the proceeds and finances of our oil? Is the oil not under our soil? Are those people from our community? Yet we have no voice. Then you will tell me that there is justice."

"You are right, my brother. We are voiceless in the face of this gross injustice and may be seriously dealt with if we decide to push hard. Those who are already neck-deep in it will do anything to keep it but I know it will not be forever."

"Yes, that is why our immediate focus is on the current challenge. I tell you, this is where the trouble will start."

A dismayed Oyiga returned without fish, to the disappointment of his buyers. Whenever such a misfortune occurred, the fish traders explored another riverine community quite distinct from the polluted area, preferably upstream. Ordinarily, on his return Oyiga and his wife usually cut the fish into chunks, cleared the bowels and placed them on a grill resting over smouldering wooden racks.

---

"What is the matter with Yiga and his wife? Are you sure they are sane?" One of Oyiga's community members wanted to know.

"They must be covering up a lot of their pains with this fish business, otherwise how can they appear to be okay with just one daughter? One grown daughter, and fish, nothing more," responded another.

Oyiga and Rita would rather wait for providence, after medical reports had declared them fit. They cherished the company of each other and this was as surprising as it was rare in a community where love was just a matter of rhetoric and what mattered was the ability to co-habit, copulate and produce offspring.

Naminsa had a strong male descent system of property ownership. Community property was shared according to the number of male offspring in a household. So Oyiga never got more than one portion of any property shared and that portion was for him alone since there was no other male person in his household. This bothered him quite a bit and made him wonder how insensitive a people and their practices could be; how no thought what so ever was spared for his daughter's upkeep and for her, as a person, like her male counterparts.

Oyiga's elder brother's sympathy turned to anger, then to concern for Oyiga and his perceived stubbornness. Idiapa had talked to his brother countless times on this issue and each time, Oyiga had calmed him with gentle words. After another encounter that received the same manner of response, he relentlessly advised his brother one more time.

"Yiga, if your wife is not capable, please pick another from our wholesome collection of young females. Every man needs sons."

"Bro, please give me more time. I believe that what will be, will be. I do not know why my life is the way it is but I know that people are destined differently. Just give me some more time, please."

Oyiga's philosophical stance made his brother wonder about his kind of person. Feeling that his entreaties had fallen on deaf ears, Idiapa gave up on his brother and aligned his thoughts with those of the people, that his brother might indeed have become insane or bewitched.

Rita was shocked when Remane, her confidant and one of the community school teachers, told her what some people in the community said about her. Although most people derided and tagged them the couple that preferred fish to children, some were more understanding.

"It is just unfortunate that people never mind their business. Everyone is not meant to be the same or go through the same process of living," said Remane, in company of some of her colleagues in the staff room of her school, when the issue came up.

"But at least one more would not hurt," countered Imina.

"Listen, everyone has his or her own destiny and no one knows what it is. You talk as if the power to have 'one more' as you suggested lies in their hands. We have been taught that whatever happens to us on this earth is with a purpose and that the One, courtesy of whom, we are here, knows why and how everything happens. Why some have and others don't, He knows. He also knows why in this world, some have food but cannot eat, some can eat but have no food, while some have food and can eat. I think it is our holy book which says that we should give thanks in all situations because we are not in control of anything; rather we are under His control. If I die tomorrow, you would say 'oh what a sad thing'; but to the great One, it may not be such a sad thing, it could be something other than sad, as deemed fit by Him. And in any case, is earthly strife's final achievement not death? Why do we keep burdening our mind with what we might have no control over? After all, at the end of our earthly endeavour, what is ultimately reserved for us all is just a small six-feet-deep space, or as the case may be, a decent corner in the crematorium. And nobody is immune to that final assignment. So please, leave this couple alone; you don't know what tomorrow holds for them, or for you either," concluded Remane.

"Madam Preacher, we have heard you, but why don't you trade positions?" teased Tiatia, one of them, but Remane chose to ignore the comment.

# CHAPTER THREE

## *The Expedition*

"Who is the one that turns fish into sons?"
"Uncle Oyiga"
"Who is the one that turns fish into daughters?"
"Aunty Rita"
"Who is the one that makes fish her siblings?"
"Biase, fine, fine Biase, thank Goodness you are not fish."

The children clapped and sang, playing their game, thinking neither of the people they were singing about nor the meaning of what they were saying. They were merely singing a play song, as far as they were concerned. Could it be that they picked a cue from the discussions of community adults? Not realising that this could bother Oyiga and family, the community people did not caution the children. Biase's smile began to disappear but her only friend Sophie did a lot to restore it with her warm company. Sophie was her cushion against the unwarranted aggression against her.

Oyiga considered leaving home for a while, as advised by one of his fellow traders in whom he had confided.

"You see, I was married for eleven years but we did not have babies until my wife and I moved away from the environment. Within one year of our relocation, our first child arrived. We have three kids now. I don't know, but a different environment might just make the difference," Levi, his fellow fish trader said to him.

Oyiga was at the crossroads, wondering if he should relocate or stay put. He sought the opinion of his wife and daughter and they bought the idea right away, hopeful that it would give them a new lease of life. Oyiga figured that the best place to go would be where they could get fish easily and continue their business. The only place he could think of was one of the riverine areas where he and the other traders used to travel to in search of fish. They had always bought fish from the fishermen after they had emerged from water and never had cause to go on water to look for them. This time he had to take a trip to the creek community of Sosowota. It was only during this trip that he truly saw what it took to get to a fishing community. It entailed moving on water in a speed boat to get there. Oyiga wondered why as a fish dealer of his calibre he had never had a boat ride. He reminded himself that Naminsa was not a riverine location, and he had never been that adventurous. Sosowota was a small bubbling community surrounded by water and inhabited by people who appeared to have nothing more than good health attained from the variety of fish meals they consumed.

They had no electricity but the people did not seem bothered. Cool breeze was never in short supply and it was common to see men in shorts and women with only clothe wrappers around their chests sitting and drawing in dewy air. The smell of fish water oozed from the environment and people simply moved around, oblivious of the almost complete absence of infrastructure in the environment. Most of them lived in thatch tents erected on water. Oyiga imagined that Sosowota was an island as he saw water all over. He also saw fish all over and found himself smiling over that, making sure he bought as much as he could, for it was quite low priced. One thing he did not know was how the people normally reacted to the type of problem he was running away from. Oyiga hoped the people of Sosowota would at least be friendlier than his own folks. The fact that Sosowota people knew neither his family nor their history gave him a measure of confidence and made him believe that this might provide the needed break. He feared for his daughter's education though, hoping the community had good schools. The people of Sosowota ate mainly fish and drank a lot of the local gin which was highly alcoholic. They had less care than the people of Naminsa and Oyiga hoped that his wife and daughter would like his choice. He also hoped that they would be insulated from the lifestyle of Sosowota people. As for Oyiga himself, the right place has already been found. So he spent a few days there making concrete arrangements about their transfer to that community, before going back to Naminsa. On his return home, he told his wife what the journey entailed and the wife could not hide her apprehension.

"Travel on water? We don't even know how to swim," Rita said.

"We shall learn how to, as soon as we get there. Just let us get there first. In fact, everybody should know how to swim; I realised this when I took that trip on water. So I have decided that the first thing we will do when we get there is to learn to swim. I already found out that there are shallow areas where people learn to swim. Local guides are always around, ready to coach and assist beginners. I think you will like the place."

Rita stared at him, unsure she understood all he said.

"Don't worry, dear. We'll get over it; we'll be fine." He gave her a pat on the back and then went over to his elder brother's house.

"Bro Idia," Oyiga began, "I want to relocate with my family temporarily to Sosowota, a fishing creek community, far from home, where we can continue with our fish business. I have finalised arrangements for our movement and we would be taking off as soon as we exhaust our current stock."

"What do you mean? What about the issue we were talking about previously?" Idiapa reminded.

"Oh! About making babies, we can still make them there," replied Oyiga.

"I am not against your pitching your business tent anywhere but I advise you to take a new wife, move to the new location with her and perhaps leave Rita and Biase here, so you'll give her your full attention, you know what I mean." Idiapa gave out a dry smile.

"That is a good suggestion, Bro Idiapa, but we are already set to go. We just need a little break. It will be for a short while, I promise and who knows, Rita might return with pregnancy or babies; you never can tell."

Idiapa simply shrugged his shoulders, satisfied that he had done his best.

# CHAPTER FOUR

# The Escape Bid

Within the next few days, Oyiga and his family took off. Rita packed a moderate baggage for a start, since this was like the introductory visit; Biase too. Oyiga could not be bothered with any luggage; he only took one or two shirts and trousers with a few other personal effects which he carried in a small bag. They travelled by road to the point where they had to continue on water.

On sighting water, Rita whispered to her husband how scared she was. Biase dragged her feet. Oyiga played the man and pretended not to be scared. He convinced himself he could do it, after all he had done it before. Men, women and their younger ones stood, chatting gaily, on a queue ready to embark on the boat ride. Biase looked at all the people around the waterside and wondered where they were all headed. Some of the people stepped into other boats, while others stepped out. Oyiga collected their tickets and they stepped into a speed boat and sat down. Biase had never had a boat ride before. She saw several people who could be classified as her peers and became more forward looking.

When he got the required number of passengers, Kruso, the boat operator, turned on the ignition and sped off. Rita and Biase froze on their seats but they later began to feel good as the boat moved steadily, splashing water in its trail. Biase thought that was quite interesting. She looked all around, watching other fast moving boats in the distance and slow moving canoes. An array of boats and canoes littered the surface of the water and moving in different directions.

They squinted through to the bright blue sky. The bright power of sunlight did not permit a direct look. The atmosphere lured Biase into forgetting her fright. She looked upwards and sideways, slowly savouring the excitement the trip brought her. Boats sped ahead to the stretching shores of another community, which appeared to be the base of several oil company expatriates. Biase got carried away, looking at an elegant Caucasian female expatriate walking leisurely on the beach, catching the glance of many. She thought she saw the woman's foot prints on the wet beach sand, as her long and beautiful legs paced along. She wore on her left leg, some exquisite Morrocan ankle beads that caught Biase's fancy. The young girl, who had never seen ankle beads before, was glad to note that some other passengers were watching as well, with interest. The sun, as if playing a trick on them, gradually hid itself and after sometime surfaced again, as if with a smile. Biase looked ahead and saw a stretch of water without end. She looked up and saw a spread of sky without end and wondered what was it that was holding the sky, as it looked suspended. Where does the water start from and where does it end? She looked around her and saw excited people and others who appeared indifferent all in one speed boat, heading towards the same location. Some had slept off.

The sun sneaked into the cloud and hid itself again. Biase looked on. She seemed to be enjoying the affair between sun and cloud, but the sun this time appeared reluctant to re-emerge from behind the cloud. The power of the cloud over the sun manifested in minor gloom and the passengers expected brightness shortly when the hide and seek game would have been over. As their expectation mounted, the gloom deepened and gently encircled the sky, and shadowed the sun and the cloud. Large waves of gusty wind lashed at the boat and it rocked. Some of the passengers panicked. It rocked again, more fiercely and most of the passengers visibly fidgeted and asked the helmsman what was going on.

"Make una no worry, no problem. Small time everyting go stop," the helmsman muttered words of encouragement to the passengers as he fiddled with the boat's engine.

By now, most of the passengers screamed uncontrollably. As the boat rocked more and more, the good swimmers on board began to dive into water, causing the boat to rock even more. The screams heightened and attracted the people in other boats, who apparently did not have newcomers screaming like Biase and her mother. The other boats, in spite of the gloomy situation, headed to the direction of Kruso's boat, and as if some heavyweight came on the boat, it capsized. Most of the passengers swam in search of safety. It was obvious that Oyiga, Rita and Biase needed help. Some people from the other boats dived into water to help. Kruso, confused, rushed first to save Oyiga, who was splattering water, all around him but soon left him for no known reason and approached his wife who was almost sinking. In his confusion he also left her and swam fiercely towards drowning Biase. He quickly helped her on to his back and swam back to the direction of Oyiga but could not find him. Perhaps the other boat men had rescued him, he thought as he sighted Rita's head far off being washed in and out of water by the waves. Biase still clamped on to his back, water gushing from her mouth and nose, he dived towards the direction he sighted Rita's head. Kruso was unaware that one of the distant speed boats was coming to assist in the rescue operation after the occupants had sighted Rita drowning. He felt relieved at the sight of the speed boat and a boat man who dived into water from the boat and reached out to the woman. She did not respond. He pulled up her already sinking heavy body, beckoning at the others to come over and assist him. They lifted her up heavily, shaking their heads in regret and throwing her into their boat before speeding off in search of the man they had seen sinking. They combed the water but could not find him; so they headed for the nearest shore where they laid Rita on the sand, wondering what next to do. Just then, Rita moved one leg and the men were startled.

"She dey alive oh!" screamed one of them "Quick, press im back." As they applied pressure to her back, they expelled water from her body and she began to breathe faintly, but her whole body looked wan.

"Hmm, this woman im God no sleep at all," exclaimed one of them.

"Me I dey doubt whether she go fit survive reach tomorrow, she don almost quench nah, hey. Una sure say no be time we dey waste so?

We don try for am oh, make we dey go abeg. If God say she no go die, she no go die. Me I wan go o, work dey," added another, who appeared to be in a hurry to leave. They withdrew and dispersed, convinced that they had done their best, having little or no means to help further, in the complete and unfortunate absence of official government rescue operation.

Kruso was now swimming gently towards the shore, shaking his head slowly and hoping that by the next day he would find out more about the whereabouts of Biase's parents. Just as he stepped out of water, he felt the suppleness of Biase's body pressed against his back. He lifted the girl gently on to the sandy ground and dived back into the river. He had sighted his speed boat circling on a spot with the engine making a funny sound. He swam towards it and held on to it, switching off the engine. Then giving it gentle pushes, he swam on behind it, to the shore. Some of his passengers who had swum ashore were already either sitting or lying on the sand. They all sympathised greatly with Biase, amid noises, hushed talks. A little while now on the shore, the people had regained control of themselves and the situation and had begun to disperse. Kruso stood akimbo, on the shore, facing the vast expanse of water and looking far, searching the water with his eyes, as if looking for something. He could not account for two passengers. He shook his head and slowly walked to the shore office to report the loss.

"Oh my God, how I wish they had life jackets. I am just a poor boatman; I cannot afford life jackets for my passengers. Besides, most people who cruise with us know how to swim. Several who do not know how to swim have done the journey many times with us without hiccups. I just don't understand today's tragedy. Oh my God, why didn't that man kit his family with life jacket? They appeared naïve and vulnerable." Kruso lamented. He had arranged for the other passengers to be conveyed to their destination; and not knowing what to do with Biase, decided to take her to his family compound at Pionto, where everybody was full of pity for the poor girl. Kruso's mother quickly prepared hot fresh fish pepper soup which they persuaded Biase to take, but the young girl had become too traumatised to eat. She took only a few spoonfuls and could not continue. They showed her a place where she took a hot bath and handed her some warm clothing.

Kruso made intermittent checks on Biase to ensure that she was fine and reported back to the rest of his family. They had to be sure that the girl was alright and that no aftermath syndrome affected her. People had been known to die in their sleep after being rescued from drowning. A little after midnight when everyone else had gone to bed, Kruso went to have a last check on his guest before going to bed. One more glance at the sleeping black beauty and the memory of the softness of Biase's body became vivid in his imagination. He closed his eyes and wondered how *sweet* the damsel would *taste*. Home advantage on his side, his masculine arsenal stiffened, and with every other person asleep, the stage was set for Kruso to do as he pleased. He hurriedly stripped the girl, who was fast asleep and immediately went into her. Tired, Biase stirred, uttered a faint cry, slowly opening her eyes and closing them again. She was aware that somebody was tampering with her body and dimly saw Kruso but was too weak and too sleepy to scream, even though she felt pain. Kruso finished up and stepped out of the room. Heading towards his own room, he fell and uttered a deep piercing cry that woke the household and got them running to him. He had just been bitten by a deadly snake. According to the people's belief, that snake, the Minja snake, only acted when there was evil around. In their confusion, they applied their popular snake bite antidote known as minjadiete to Kruso's leg and also mixed some in water for him to drink.

# CHAPTER FIVE

# Justice from Minja

Kruso's mother was the first to come out. The episode of the previous day had almost given her a restless night.

"Good morning, Mama," someone greeted from behind her.

"Good morning, child," she responded turning to a vibrant youth of the compound. "Sumi dear, I am still shaken by what happened yesterday but I am glad we have a hero in the person of Kruso, although I still fear for the life of that young girl."

"Mama, the girl will be fine, since she did not die hours after the accident. I think she will be fine."

"I am sure that Kruso is still exhausted from all the hard work of yesterday. I need him to check on his patient and give me feedback. I am worried."

"Hey Kruso, the people's Kruso! Kruso, the hero, wake up and feed Mama back on your pretty patient!" Sumi hailed, trying to get Kruso out of his room.

No answer.

"Mama, your delicious pepper soup of last night appears to be working overtime in his body." Sumi gave out a roaring laughter and with Mama, decided to give Kruso more time. Kruso's mother returned to her chores and Sumi sauntered to the grounds beyond the family compound, where he mingled with other community boys. One hour had passed and Kruso's mother had finished warming the left-over food for breakfast. She scooped out a bit and tasted it.

"Hmm, overnight food sabi sweet well well. No wonder Kruso like am plenty." She walked towards Kruso's room and slapped her palm on the door.

"Kruso-eh, no let food cold o, come chop." She went back to her room.

Kruso must have heard her, she thought. No need to disturb him further. Then she heard knocks on her door.

"Good morning o. I hope say una sleep well. Mama Kruso, we hear about last night o. As I come out, naim I meet Lovet for road as she dey come too."

"Good morning, Elfrida, Lovet, una morning. Two of una this morning eh? Una welcome."

"How Kruso dey now? We hear say Ninja bite am," Lovet spoke.

"Na true, my sister, but we don give am the follow-treatment," Kruso's mother responded, just as Sumi and his friends strolled into the compound, to see Kruso. She called out to Sumi.

"Go call am out nah, tell am say people come to see am. Hin chop sef dey cold."

Kruso was not in a position to see any of them. Sumi found him lifeless after he kicked open the door to his room. The brightness of that morning had turned out not to be for Kruso's people. Kruso, a surviving twin of his mother, lay stone dead on his bed. Anger and confusion greeted the people. They had woken up to yet another tragedy; this time, their own tragedy. There was pandemonium, wailing and cursing. Biase was still deeply asleep, as if drugged, oblivious of happenings around her. A little patch of blood mixed with some creamy substance had dried up between her thighs, as she slumbered.

"It is that strange girl that my son brought to us from the river; she must be a witch or a river personality. Can't you see that her mere presence has proved enough to stir up Minja? Oh Kruso, why didn't you allow that water spirit to drown in the river? See what she has caused; I am finished. Years back, I lost Krumo, now it is Kruso. O my dear twins! What am I living for-eh? Kruso tell me, what am I living for? Oh Kruso! Kruso! Heeey!" Kruso's mother cried, pacing about hysterically in their small clustered compound. The women tried to hold her hands in a bid to console her but she slipped off their grip on to the ground and rolled on the dirt ground.

"Yes, she may even have caused the death of her own parents, and now Kruso's. She must have caused the boat mishap. Let's send her away before she causes more havoc," suggested Kruso's uncle who immediately made a swift move to the room where Biase was still sleeping and angrily pulled her up, asking her who she really was. Others were also swift in joining him. Biase moped at them. They just did not know what to do with her as they were not even sure how much more powers they thought she possessed. Only her tears spoke for her. She nodded when asked if she could lead the way to her hometown. Before even talking about burying Kruso, the people wanted to make sure they had done away with the person they considered the evil one in their midst. So they took Biase right back to Naminsa.

Her people could neither believe their ears nor eyes but Biase confirmed the story and her people's grief knew no bounds. The community absorbed their shock and thanked the visitors for all the trouble and sent two men with them up to the Pionto shore office to take care of all the other issues concerning the tragedy. Before leaving, the visitors dropped an angry hint that it was not impossible that their daughter Biase could possess some evil powers and urged them to be watchful.

"How could that be? She is only a young girl, a prudent girl who did not exhibit any evil traits. Not Biase! What you are saying is quite shocking but we'll keep our eyes on the ground, despite the more shocking problem we have at hand."

"Yes, please do, because nothing happens for nothing. You know they say the toad does not run in the day time for nothing. The man who rescued your daughter died mysteriously the same night she was rescued. For someone who performed such a heroic act to just die like that beats the imagination," one of the visitors said, shaking his head.

"Oh really, how sad! We are sorry to hear about that. We'll try and find out what went wrong. We'll surely do. Something must be the matter."

Three days after the boat mishap, Oyiga's body was found floating but there was no trace of Rita. The Naminsa men took home their kinsman's corpse. With heavy heart, Idiapa took the lead in the funeral of his younger brother. The community was thrown into grief. Biase moved in with the family of Idiapa. Everything in her life had come to a stop, except for the little movement she began to feel inside her. Few months went by and her belly really began to protrude. Biase's uncle's wife was alarmed at what she noticed and promptly drew her husband's attention to it.

Her uncle figured that he now had another tragedy on his hands and decided to avert it, his own way. Biase's uncoordinated story of a man coming over her in her sleep and that of the snake bite and the death of the aggressor was regarded as balderdash. It was the only truth she knew, so she maintained it.

"She must have been pregnant here before travelling with her parents," Idiapa said to no one in particular.

He asked her again and she told the same story. He just could not take it. "Look here Biase!" her uncle yelled. "I am sure you know who got you pregnant. You will just quietly go back to him and save us from this disgrace. You must not remain here by sunset."

"Uncle, I swear, this happened in…"

"Shut up, you liar! You want to tell me that it happened in water? Is that what you want us to believe? You pretentious liar! I am off now and if by the time I come back you are still here, then, I will not be held responsible for any action I take." He stormed out of the house, leaving Biase and his wife there.

"Aunty, I was so weak on that…" Biase tried to explain to her uncle's wife but she interrupted her.

"Look, young lady, I do not intend to interfere in your problem with your uncle, please. Just keep me out of it. But remember, your uncle meant every word he said." Biase nearly wept blood. She remembered her parents, particularly her mother.

"Oh, Mother! My mummy! Where are you? Where are you Mother?" She sobbed as she packed the few clothes she had left, into an old travel bag, ready to go, only God knows where.

She needed someone to talk to, so she went to her friend, Sophie. Sophie did her best to have a good chat with her, to work her up to a better mood. They both agreed that the Sister's Home was the best place to seek assistance.

"If you stay here, your uncle will come with his palaver."

"I know, Sophie. It is not even the best to remain in the community. I will die of shame. Sophie, please help me out."

"Don't worry," Sophie consoled, "whenever I am hard up, my mother always says to me: 'it will pass'; and whenever she says it, she repeats it in French, 'ça passera'. You know she understands and speaks French, and I tell you, I have watched the way things happen, they have always passed. So, take it easy for this one will also pass. I will accompany you to the Sisters' Home and will make sure I pay you regular visits there, until it passes. Don't worry, stop crying, I believe your story. Can't you see that the man has already been punished? In fact, the punishment for rape should be death, period!" Sophie cursed.

# CHAPTER SIX

# The Raboni Home

With an old bag containing her belongings and Sophie by her side, she called out at a commercial motorbike rider and asked him to take them to the Raboni Home for the Underprivileged. The home is run by Reverend Sisters seven kilometers away. They both squeezed into the space behind the bike man and were soon at the Home. There, Biase in tears narrated her ordeal to the sisters who gave her a listening ear and asked piercing questions to which she gave frank answers. The sisters, in their usual manner, wrote down everything Biase said. They were alarmed that a man could after performing such an act of kindness, also fall into such a sinful act of cruelty. They agreed to accommodate her, with a promise to nurse her pregnancy till full term. The Home usually received adolescent girls who by mistake or coercion were carrying circumstantial pregnancies but who were not considering the option of abortion.

Outside the Home, after Biase's case had been sorted out and she had been given a place, the two friends got locked in a long embrace, after which Sophie hurried home on another bike, in order to get home before sunset. Thereafter, she paid Biase regular visits as promised, sometimes taking along some snacks and definitely, community news and gossip.

"Biase, can you imagine that back home they are saying that you killed your parents, and the man who rescued you, returned and then ran away from home."

"That's exactly what those Kruso's people told them. Oh my God, how can I make them understand that it is not true? Sophie, why am I so unlucky? Where did they say I ran to?"

"They don't quite know your whereabouts. You know, the news of your pregnancy surprisingly has not spread perhaps because the tragedy and its cause were still dominating discussions."

"It could also be because my uncle and his wife do not want to answer questions about my whereabouts. If they open their mouths wide and spread news about the pregnancy, people will definitely ask where they had sent me to and they'd be at a loss as to what reply to give them."

"I think you are right, Biase."

Biase learnt to accommodate both sides of what her friend's visit brought. She wondered but imagined that if she had the powers, she would have killed Kruso herself, with her bare hands. The Reverend Sisters loved Biase and liked her sheer intelligence and simplicity. She enrolled in the Home's academic and spiritual classes while her pregnancy progressed.

One of the Raboni Sisters, Callista, was a native of the riverine area, where the boat mishap happened. Another Sister Konsolina, having been raped in her younger days by two carefree youths in her village, before she became a nun, took particular interest in Biase. The masked boys had waylaid and dragged her into the bush, blindfolding her. Then they raped her to their satisfaction, one after the other. Since nobody else knew about it and she did not even see her assailants, she kept quiet and decided to serve in the Lord's vineyard. After jotting down Biase's story, Sister Konsolina locked up herself in a room and wept bitterly. Whenever she looked at Biase, she saw herself and thanked God that her own assault did not result in pregnancy. For these Sisters, the Convent had become home as they totally belonged there and could only pay short scheduled visits to their native homes. Stories of boats capsizing and people drowning were not strange to both of them, so also were stories of pollution from oil residue destroying crustaceans and amphibians. Sister Callista told Biase that whenever that happened, the people suffered a great deal and became angry with the powers-that-be. She told her that it usually took a long time for aquatic life to get restored. Biase remembered the story her father came home with when they could not find fish to buy in the creeks. She recalled that her daddy came back empty-handed and talked about dead fish floating on the surface of water. It was all similar to what Callista was explaining to her and appeared to be a regular occurrence.

---

It was Sister Callista's brother's wedding and she paid a short visit to her native community to attend the solemnisation of the union between her brother Paul and his heartthrob Marian.

"The Lord has answered my prayer; I will sing praises to Him
Answer eh, eh, eh, Answer eh, eh, eh, oh Lord"

The choir sang with joy. The moderate accompaniment added a pleasant touch to the music and made it very flattering to the ear. One song after another, the choir and the congregation kept the church alive until Fr. Damian emerged from the vestry where the marriage register had just been signed by the couple. He raised his right hand and the singing stopped. The couple and a short entourage had also come out of the church vestry. The redness of the bride's eyes was a clear indication that she had cried over signing off her maiden name and her eventual transfer to another family.

"The Lord, be with you," Fr. Damian said.

"And also with you!" the congregation responded, and he asked the couple to come directly in front of the congregation, while he stood aside and said in a loud voice:

"Brethren, may I introduce to you the latest couple in town, today, Mr. Paul and Mrs. Marian Igirigi."

The bride's mother jumped from her seat onto the aisle and did a small graceful dance, shouting and waving her right arm, "Praaaiisse the Lord!"

"Hallelujah!" resounded from the congregation.

"As I said earlier, what God has put together, let no man or woman put asunder, in Jesus' name!"

"Amen!"

"Offering time!" the priest had announced.

"Blessing time!" the congregation chorused.

"Come forward and be blessed," Fr. Damian said, gesticulating with his hands to the worshippers. Then turning to the choir, he raised his hand again and the choir's sweet rendition filled the air once more.

Tuwara Ya nmanma

Tuwara Ya nmanma

Si Ya n'O mee na

Si Ya n'O mee na

Eze Jisos, tuwara Ya nmanma

Si Ya n'O mee na

Row by row, the congregation danced to the altar with their thanks offering, feeling joyous. Shortly after, the priest gave the closing blessing.

By a corner outside the church, the sweet smell of flowers mingled with the joy of the day, as the click of cameras targeted smiling faces. Sister Callista walked up to Fr. Damian.

"Thanks Fr. for the wonderful homily. It was devoid of the usual threats that made marriage look so burdensome and scary to some."

"You are welcome, Sister. A proper marriage should not be scary at all. It is a blessing where God's wonder is made manifest, where one plus one becomes one. No wonder our Master began his miraculous manifestation at a wedding ceremony. It is meant to be blissful and society must not make it seem otherwise." Father Damian grabbed the right hand of Sister Callista and asked in a solemn manner. "How is the mission at the convent?"

"Very well Fr. Thank you."

"Glory to Jesus!" he said as he raised his hands.

"Honour to Mary!" Callista placed her two palms together.

They both made the sign of the cross and Sister Callista departed, giving way to the teeming parishioners waiting to exchange greetings with Father Damian.

Sister Callista was away for one week but to Biase it felt like six months. Sister Konsolina never allowed any gap though. She had chatted up Biase, and made sure she did not slip into the sour memory of her ordeal.

Sister Konsolina had a way of keeping tab of happenings in the Home in such a way that she did not allow things to go awry. She did not talk much but spoke a lot of sense whenever she did. Biase wished she could spend as much time with her as with Sister Callista but unknown to Biase, labour in the Home was appropriately divided, and taking care of Biase fell within Callista's assignment. Sister Konsolina performed a general oversight on the entire Home. Sister Callista did not talk much either but is filled with smiles and gentility; the Home knew this fact and that was why they assigned new entrants to her, aware that she possessed the qualities that could calm even a demon.

The sisters had their own meals only after other residents had finished eating and Biase was marvelled to note that the food given to other resident was sometimes more delicious than the one the sisters ate. Both Sisters Konsolina and Callista and the other sisters had decided to sacrifice all earthly pleasures for chastity, poverty and obedience. On her return Callista brought back some fable making the rounds in her hometown, of a pregnant woman who was rescued half drowned, half dead in a boat mishap months ago. She had been picked up and hospitalised at the Shores 2 oil company clinic where she was recuperating. People who went to see her at the clinic came with the information that the woman had inhaled and swallowed a lot of water, coupled with excessive breeze from the waves and these had affected her speech and hearing but that she was rapidly responding to treatment. The woman's pregnancy, according to the women who went to see her, should be about six months old.

"Poor woman, some are lucky, others are not. Where are her people?"

"That is the problem. No one knows her; she does not belong to any of the neighbouring communities. People just visit the hospital to see a supposed dead woman who was revived at the oil company hospital; a pregnant woman. They said she was in coma for, many days and when she woke up, it was discovered that she had serious health problems as a result of her ordeal," Replied Callista.

"Oh, I wish her luck. I pray that her people find her soon, at least because of the baby she is carrying," Biase added. She closed her eyes and in a moment relived the experience of that day, seeing her father drown and learning that her mother was picked up supposedly dead. Kruso saw those who picked her shaking their heads in pity. Biase recollected what happened in Kruso's home and hot streaming tears flowed from her eyes.

Callista drew close to her, wiping her tears and asked, "Could that be your mother, Biase?"

"No," sobbed Biase, "they picked her lifeless and, besides, Mum was not pregnant."

"I am sorry. Please stop crying, I just thought about you when they told the story at home. Maybe there is no connection. Come, let's take a walk."

# CHAPTER SEVEN

## The he-Goat

Life continued at the Raboni's with Biase and the other occupants, some of whom were brought in due to extreme destitution. Some were orphans, some displaced and others elderly. A few months after Biase arrived at the Raboni's, one little girl was brought in. She was called Jennifer and aged between 13 and 14. Sonnie, her aunty's husband, had impregnated her. Sonnie had been married to Rosemary for over seven years. Jennifer was the little girl Rosemary brought from the village to the city where they resided, to assist her with household chores. She was about eight years old when she came to live with them and had lived with them for about five years. Sonnie abused her regularly for several months and threatened to kill her if she ever said anything to Madam. The man Sonnie had lost his job and claimed to be searching for another. So whenever his wife, a nurse, was about to go to work leaving Jennifer to look after their youngest child, the man also got prepared and ensured that they went out together. But he always came back shortly after and remained at home for the rest of the day. He had an odd job with Jennifer till Madam found out after she retrieved a forgotten pair of juvenile underwear from beneath a pillow in the bedroom. The husband swore he had never seen any such thing before and suggested it might have been brought in by their other children. His wife pretended to buy her husband's story but called Jennifer aside and told her that her husband had told her everything.

"I just want to thank you for being such a good girl and for allowing my husband to touch and sleep with you, when I am not around. He told me and I was happy," Rosemary teased.

Jennifer nodded and the lid was blown off the can. She thereafter narrated, on Rosemary's prompting, every detail of Sonnie's atrocious behaviour. Rosemary nearly went berserk. Sonnie denied everything but Rosemary, bent on finding out the truth, took Jennifer to a doctor, who in the course of examining the girl discovered that she was not only abused, but also pregnant. That was just too much for Rosemary to handle so she took the case to their kinsmen back home. The kinsmen, in settling the matter, never openly blamed Sonnie. All they did was ask Rosemary what the matter was, and after she had told them, they called the girl to hear from her but never questioned the 'lord'. No one even asked him if it was true or not that he abused the little girl put in his care.

"What happened has happened and it is unfortunate that it happened the way it did. We must find a quick solution to it. I suggest that Sonnie could, at the worst, take the girl as second wife. The oil has already been spilled," said one of the kinsmen and, turning to Rosemary, continued: "Our dear wife, I appeal to you not to take it too much to heart. Please try and accept the girl if your husband decides to marry her."

Rosemary left that meeting, sorry for her people, her country and their customary values, norms and judgment.

"This is why wives shoot husbands to death in some parts of the developed world. What nonsense! As a matter of fact, I feel like shooting that he-goat to death. It's unfortunate that in this part of the world, things happen differently."

Her blood boiled within her and streamed out in form of tears from her eyes. Seeing the man around her made her feel like throwing up. Her only other alternative was to ask him to leave her home. They lived in one of the nurses' apartments allocated to her as a senior nurse. Rosemary continued with her work and tried to put behind her what had happened. Within her people's traditional setup, it would amount to a taboo if she sued her husband or sought litigation, even with the kangaroo judgment the elders carried out. She must accept her lot and endure whatever came her way in marriage but Rosemary had just gone

against the norm and committed a major sin by asking her husband to leave her official quarters. She felt some relief when the man left. When her friend, Evelyn, told her that what she did was wrong, she almost swayed but remembered that it was between her life and her death.

"Evli," she called out to her friend. "What would you feel if I died now?"

"God forbid it. What will kill you? Who will kill you? Please don't talk that way."

"You didn't even know that by sending Sonnie away, I was able to at least save myself from a suicide bid. I simply removed the cause. Thanks to my job, I am able to cope. I saw no better option because if I had allowed him to stay, and did not commit suicide, that would have meant me dying of frustration, gradually. It is that bad; I was that hurt."

"But you have incurred the wrath of the elders of the community because they viewed your decision as atrocious and abominable. Their female counterparts, the daughters of the land, will team up with them and wait for you to visit home."

"It should at least make them happy that whatever wrath they want to unleash would not be on a corpse. Evli, please let's focus on other issues. Pray that you do not have a similar experience."

Rosemary sent Jennifer to the Raboni's. Everyone cursed the man who did that to her. Biase was happy that attention had shifted to Jennifer. Biase thought that Jennifer looked like a baby. It was inconceivable to her that Jennifer was pregnant, especially as there was no visible sign of it to Biase's adolescent eyes. The Sisters always saw and handled different cases, providing succour to the afflicted. They sent Jennifer to the special care unit, which was like a juvenile section and she had little or no interaction with older people. They provided her with books and play materials that could aid her learning process.

Time went by and Rosemary's anger waned. She came more regularly to check on Jennifer, taking along some grocery, each time. But she still blocked out Sonnie from her immediate memory. Sophie's visit to Biase never waned; her visit provided the opportunity for both friends to avail themselves the goodness of each other's company. Biase's belly was bigger now and she experienced distinct movements of life in her belly. She and Sophie listened and felt this movement whenever she came around.

# CHAPTER EIGHT

## The Fairy Tale

One day Callista's brother, Paul, visited the Raboni's to see his sister and thank her once more for the sisterly role she played during his wedding. A happy Sister Callista called out all her friends to come and see her brother at the lobby. She bought some soft drinks and snacks from the canteen and they ate and drank as they chatted. Biase noticed that Callista's brother kept casting intermittent glances at her and wondered what he was up to, but they all chatted till Paul got up to leave.

"Who is that pregnant lady, Calli?" he asked

"Oh, she is a resident. Why do you ask Paul? Remember you just got married and besides, that girl is pregnant and I do not understand your interest in her."

"Easy now, sister, ah, I have not said I am interested in her. I am just being curious, and in any case, no harm in asking. But she is very cute sha and her dark complexion stands her out."

"My brother, please leave that girl alone. She's been through hell. How is Marian? I hope she is coping fine with married life?"

"Oh yes, we are doing our best, thank you." Paul paused for a moment then continued, "Calli, do you mean that the girl got that pregnancy from hell or are you saying that pregnancy is hell? Well, maybe hell preceded by paradise eh? But I want to know..."

"Enough of that banter," said Callista, piqued by Paul's insensitivity and indirect verbal assault on Biase's personality. "Look, Paul, I dislike you when you talk in a carefree manner. That girl! Boat mishap survivor, rape victim, pregnant, homeless, haba, that's too much for one girl; and there you are making sarcastic comments. Is that fair?"

"Well, I didn't know, but I don't believe everything I hear and think. You should also always verify issues. Is it possible for one person to be linked with this number of misfortunes you just listed? Anyway, there is something about her that I cannot explain. That's what prompted me to ask about her. I think I should be going now."

"Okay now, have a safe trip back and send my regards to those at home," Sister Callista bade him farewell, happy that the lewd discussion had come to an end.

At the Shores Clinic 2, Doctor Stapyioth sat by a woman's bed holding her hand. The oil companies operating in the creeks had recently opened clinics and cottage hospitals in the area for the communities, and numbered them as they were opened. The Shores clinic 2 was the second to be opened and the woman had the privilege of being looked after there, by a team led by Dr. Stapyioth.

"How are you feeling today?"

He sought to know, out of formality. He already knew that she had recovered as all the tests had shown. Her chest had become clear, her blocked ear opened and the slur in her speech disappearing. She had regained her appetite and her beautiful dark and undiluted complexion had blossomed once more. The doctor took a long look at this woman and, imagining what would have happened to her had they not intervened, shook his head slowly.

"I am fine, doctor. Thank you," she replied, giving the doctor a healthy smile.

"Good, very good. The scan result shows that you are over seven months pregnant." The woman looked at the doctor, surprised and pensive. She looked at her belly and then at the doctor again. "And you are carrying twins and they are in good condition." Doctor Stapyioth told her, nodding and smiling, looking into her eyes.

That appeared to be too much news at a time for her and she voiced out her deep surprise.

"Seven months, twins, how Doctor, how? Can that be possible?" She queried slowly, gently rubbing her belly with her hands, trying to feel the supposed pregnancy.

"You must have been pregnant before that accident. You have been here for over four months now, and that means the pregnancy was almost three months old then. Don't you remember missing your period before the trip?"

"Doctor, I don't know. I was too busy and tensed up to notice anything then. I was miserable and had lost confidence in myself so much that I did not believe I was capable of ever taking in again. I was neither counting nor checking but I remember now that for some time before the trip, I did not buy sanitary towels. Okay, I did not have my monthly period but it did not mean anything to me. In fact I did not quite notice anything, I am not sure… I just noticed that my belly had grown big and thought the water I swallowed was moving inside of me and taking some time to clear from my system. Oh my God! How can I be pregnant and my husband will never know about it? Something we longed for together. Oh how sweet it would have been to witness and cherish it together." Looking straight into the doctor's eyes, she asked, "Still nothing of him has been heard?"

The doctor slowly shook his head.

"And my daughter, my only child, nothing heard of her?"

"Listen, madam, I don't want you to start again. We've been through this several times and each time it does not lead us anywhere. I thought you should be grateful to God for sparing your live and your pregnancy. Look, you are going to have twins, in two months' time! Doesn't that make you happy? Come on, give me that smile again," Dr. Stapyioth said, pressing her hand and extracting a smile from her, in spite of tear-drops on her face.

"That's my girl," the doctor said and, still holding her hand, told her to learn to put everything behind her and look forward to returning to her natural home, promising that they would stand by her throughout her trying period and accompany her to her home community in due time. The hospital management knew that they had to be careful not to discharge her from hospital and let her be immediately on her own. She was their miracle patient whose case tested their professional expertise and medical competence and proved them a force to reckon with. The treatment and care given to her also was to prove that they cared for community life and were giving back to the community. This was in response to the criticism oil companies often received over purported negligence of the communities where they worked. Rita Silas was benefiting from this largesse. They had plans to assist in rehabilitating her. Because they knew the story of the hostility her family was trying to escape from when tragedy struck, the oil company authorities developed a three-point plan for Rita's rehabilitation. The first would ensure that a good house was built and furnished for her, to which she would return after she must have been delivered of the babies. The second was to ensure that she went through the delivery process the safest way possible. Part of the second plan was to ensure that she and her babies were taken good care of until they were strong enough to go home. And the third plan was to ensure that they were safely taken home and made comfortable; and left with some money, supplies of baby food and baby products to last for over one year. With this grand plan finalised, Rita was like a fairy tale character and the oil company authorities like the Fairy.

# CHAPTER NINE

# The Striking Resemblance

Paul, Callista's brother, battled with the unsure feeling that the pregnant girl he saw at the Raboni's could have a correlation with the much talked about pregnant woman at Shores 2. He decided to find out more, especially as it seemed that there was a missing link; and besides, the resemblance, he felt was too striking. He remembered that during the first week of the accident that nearly claimed the woman's life, the story of the survival of a teenage girl who was involved in a boat accident with her parents was on everybody's lips throughout the neighbouring riverine and fishing communities. Later there was another story about a woman who was thought dead from the same boat accident but who eventually survived and was being taken care of by the oyibos. And also he had chatted with a girl who has 'been through hell', as his sister put it and who was probably in that same boat. Paul racked his brain to make sense of a fusion of the stories. People also heard about the gallant rescue and the Minja snake bite that claimed the life of the rescuer. There was equally whispers during the first few weeks of the accident about the eviction of the rescued girl. Events had already almost completely overtaken the stories now but Paul tried to recall all; and the more he did, the closer he felt to the root of the matter. He went back to the clinic and asked to see the medical director. Paul's face was not totally unfamiliar to Dr. Stapyioth because he was one of the regular callers who showed interest in the miracle woman. Paul actually was the head of a non-governmental organisation known as Female Rights Advancement Project (FRAP). FRAP wanted to engineer a behaviour change in a society that ignorantly punished and discriminated against female persons, from the cradle to the grave, for no reason other than that they were females. When FRAP heard that an abandoned and dying woman was picked up from the shores by expatriate oil company yachters and hospitalised at the Shores Clinic 2, they saw the need to visit the clinic and monitor the situation so that they could begin to build up a dossier on the woman, to enable them effectively carry out their obligation to the civil society and publicise the oil company's benevolence. After exchanging pleasantries, Paul went straight to the point. "I met someone – a teenage girl whom I think could be related to your patient. I mean Mrs. Silas."

"Go on. Where and how did you come about this?" Stapyioth stuttered, adjusting himself in his chair, wondering if this was not the usual gimmick of fraudsters. Paul told the doctor about his visit to the Raboni's.

"Doctor, the resemblance is striking but there is one snag, the girl too is pregnant."

"How come she is pregnant?" The doctor inquired wryly.

Paul told him that he had it on good authority that the girl was a survivor of that same accident and also a rape victim, who found her way to a Home where she was being cared for. Stapyioth had heard and seen so much since he came into the country. He had spent one and a half years already and Paul's story sounded just like one of those commonly told tales. He just looked continually at Paul as he spoke, remembering that there was something known as cock and bull story, whatever that meant, and hoping that Paul's story was not just one. But Paul was dead serious, trying to fix the jigsaw puzzle of his story right, to ensure comprehensibility.

"So what do you want?" Stapyioth asked.

"We must get these two persons to meet each other. This, I am certain, will hasten total healing on both sides and provide the vital missing link necessary for a more credible dimension of the whole story. Who knows, we might discover a veritable nest of information," Paul explained. Stapyioth remained silent, slowly taking in Paul's postulation and letting its power strengthen his own unsure stance. He was gradually digesting the following phrases: "hasten total healing", "vital missing link" and "more credible dimension". They made so much meaning that he thought Paul was a brilliant young man.

"I think you are right there, I agree with you but how do we get about it?"

Paul introduced FRAP and told him that they worked with media organisations and that FRAP can select one of them to take up the story and pursue it to its logical end.

"This method will ensure openness and across board information dissemination, using especially the radio, which is very good for community outreach. Once everything is put in place, the press will begin the sensitisation process and the relations of the victim or victims as the case may be, will become aware of the true position. This will encourage them to look for, and identify with, their missing relations. The power of the Press can never really be over-estimated." Paul enthused.

"What form will this sensitisation process take?" Dr. Stapyioth asked.

"Thank you for that question. You see, those who are familiar with mass communication know how to wade into the matter and get all sides of the story, which will be aired via the electronic media and written in the print media. People will pick it up from there, whether they are concerned or not. Those directly concerned might not even get to know, first-hand, because they may not have had access to the media. The process is usually so powerful that those who hear pass on the message to those concerned and when they hear, they rally to do something about the news. Then your good works and ours will be appropriately acknowledged."

"So what is the next step?" Stapyioth asked, really interested.

"The organisation needs to be funded to be empowered to handle this. We shall put up a proposal spelling out what we intend to do, why and how, indicating a timeline. The proposal will include a work plan and budget. We would send it to your organisation for review and possible approval, and thereafter, work will commence."

"Fine, do that and I'll table it and we'll see how it goes. OK?"

"Okay, Doc!" concluded Paul, rising and shaking hands with Dr. Stapyioth, before leaving.

## CHAPTER TEN

# The Good Samaritans

The proposal was approved and Paul set out to work, contracting a relevant media group, the Community News Network (CNN) to handle the task and make sure that no detail was left out. CNN had a crop of good journalists working for it. It operated both in rural and urban communities, covering news affecting both social and geographic communities. A crew of two reporters and one cameraman was assigned the duty, two males and one female, and they appeared happy to take on the task. The team, Mary and Clifford and Johnny, the man with the cameras, selected the Shores Clinic 2 as their first port of call. Dr. Stapyioth was pleased to take them to Rita who they introduced themselves to, and made their mission known.

"Madam, would I be wrong to say that you are one of the luckiest people living today? And if I am not wrong, Congratulations!" Mary fired the first shot, taking the lead.

"You are right my sister, thank you. I can't thank God enough," Rita cheerfully replied.

Careful not to aggravate her situation, Clifford asked questions that revealed facts about her family, their business, the accident, her survival and stay in hospital. She was close to tears again but a bit stronger now and with Clifford's gentle method, she braced up and answered every question asked, to the satisfaction of the crew. Mary came in again, giving Rita a big smile and nodding.

"Thanks a lot Madam, we must try and put the past behind us and look forward to brighter days, for the future looks indeed bright. I mean we are looking forward to your safe delivery, discharge from hospital and return home. How does that make you feel?

"Very happy even though it is going to be without my husband and daughter; but I have a strong hope of seeing my daughter again. An inner voice tells me that, all the time, that God will not leave me empty-handed."

"We have strong hope too and by the time we finish our work, we'd be hoping for the better".

"Thank you very much". She appreciated.

They talked at length with Mrs. Rita Silas, interviewing her and extracting a lot of information from her, recording her story and filming the process. Dr. Stapyioth had earlier told Rita that the exercise might help her situation, and urged her to grant the interview. Taking advantage of proximity, the crew next visited Pionto, late Kruso's village, recording and filming most of their interactions. At Pionto, they spoke chiefly to Kruso's mother and uncle, who did not want to be reminded of the strange girl whose presence attracted death to their son. Nevertheless, they answered all questions put across by the journalists. The journalists also interviewed a few other community people, who felt rather delighted at the novelty of being filmed. They posed for the camera man and made funny gesticulations. Clifford picked a young man out of the crowd for questioning.

"Hey bros, I guess you like what's going on here. Tell me, do you know about that snake bite that killed Kruso after he rescued a young girl? Do you remember the death of the rescuer himself? Do you also remember anything about the eviction of the rescued girl?"

"Yeah, I was around when it happened. You see, that snake appears only when it smells evil. It never strikes the innocent. It is unfortunate that that girl was demonised and never given an opportunity to say anything. I can bet on my life that if that girl had been guilty, Minja would have gone for her and not Kruso. Everybody got so blinded with emotion and sentiments over Kruso's death that nobody bothered to ask why it was Kruso that received the poison and not the girl. After such a heroic and kind gesture, Minja would not have killed Kruso just like that; I can bet on that but unfortunately, no one wants to find out. I pity that girl".

"Did you see the girl?"

"No I didn't. It happened at night and by morning they had sent her away. Some people only saw the sobbing girl when she was being sent away. Is it not strange for nemesis to spare the devilish and kill the angelic? Unfortunately I did not see the girl".

"So where possibly could, Kruso have gone wrong?"

"Only God knows". The man said, pointing to the sky. "One day the truth will float like cork on water, the wind will blow and we shall all see what the feathers are covering for the fowl" the young man was touched.

"Thank you for your time"

"Pleasure mine".

Later the searchlight was directed to the Raboni's, where it appeared Biase's peace was about to be disrupted. She had found so much peace and quiet, at the Raboni's that she was almost forgetting her situation. The Mary-Clifford group therefore became a prod that stirred her back to reality. She was shy to face the crew and found it difficult to open up to them but Mary called up her interpersonal and counselling skills, and applied them on her.

"My name is Mary and I am your friend." Mary had come close to her. "I'll not use anything you say against you. We are both females and it is my duty to protect you. Just trust me hmm; and see me as your very good friend, okay?" Mary gave her a gentle pat on the back and a smile, and Biase looked at her with teary eyes.

"Please can you come back some other time?" Sister Callista had said to them. Biase was simply too innocent and reserved to get into conversation with unknown interviewers on a first visit. Based on her disposition, another date was fixed for the chat. The Raboni Sisters who were watching began to talk to Biase.

"They are here in your own interest. You must put up your best and tell them all you know. You never can tell, something that might surprise you can emerge." Konsolina advised.

"Yes Biase, I am positive that this will turn out good. When they come back, please relax and have a chat with them. They are investigative journalists. Who knows, this could be the end of your trauma."

Callista added and Biase smiled demurely, nodding slowly. It was quite evident that Sisters Callista and Konsolina's counsel had prepared her further for the interview. On the appointed day she talked to the journalists, crying intermittently especially when she remembered her parents, what Kruso did to her and how her uncle had chased her away. She however refused to answer questions regarding her pregnancy and the journalists did not insist. Certain from the interviews that a correlation has been established between Rita and Biase, Mary said to her, "I can see you are crying and I can guess you must have done a lot of crying over time. You are Miss Biase Silas right?" Biase nodded, her face expressionless. "What if I tell you now that I met a woman who you resemble and whose name is Mrs. Rita Silas, will that wipe away your tears?" Instantly Biase in a reflex action rubbed her palm across her eyes. Mary asked that question, confidently looking into Biase's eyes, certain that they had found the missing link. She saw a sparkle in the girl's tearful eyes. Biase tried to find out more.

"Is it true? Did you, did you truly see her?" Mary nodded. "Is she alright? Did she ask about me? How come they said she was dead? Is she pregnant? Has she had the baby or..? Where is... where is she now and...?" Biase reeled with trepidation.

"Hey! Take it easy now, too many questions, one at a time, baby girl!" Mary teased. "Where do you want us to start from? Yes it is really true, we indeed saw her. She is fine and she asked about you. Yes she is really pregnant and might deliver in the next month or so. Don't worry, it won't be long before a meeting between the two of you is arranged and you will see for yourself that your mother is alive. They probably told you that she was dead because they thought she really was. She was actually left for dead and picked up by some good "Samaritans"... but all that is mere story now." Biase remained dazed, moping at Mary as if she was a strange spectacle.

"Can you take us to Naminsa? We want to have a chat with your uncle and others there," Clifford requested, opening up an old wound and touching a sore point. Ever since she left her uncle's house, after being disgracefully sent away, Biase had not returned there and was not in a position to go back with the crew, not even on a short visit. She was not even sure if her uncle tried to look for her, even for one day. She calmly declined and rather gave them a clear direction on how to get there and who to ask for. Thanking Biase and the Raboni Sisters, the group left and Biase could not describe what she felt: something between happiness and confusion but with no known name under the sky. Although sleep eluded her that night, tears were not hard to find and were not in short supply either, just like the several thoughts that coursed her mind. When she managed to sleep, she had a dream in which she met her mother and tried to give her a hug but their two protruding bellies proved a big obstacle so both of them decided to hug sideways. She woke up and could not go back to sleep, scared that the dream could mean that the whole exercise was a sham.

The visit to Naminsa took a dramatic turn when after exchange of greetings and introductions, Clifford told Idiapa, Oyiga's brother that they had come to make inquiries about Oyiga's family. That was the shot that stirred the hornet's nest.

"What do you want to know about a dead man? He is dead and buried. We could not find his wife's corpse. What else do you want or are you going to bring him back to life?" Idiapa paused for a while and scrutinised them adding, "Are you sure you are not spies? Who sent you here? We don't need any of you, go away from here." He charged at the cameraman, "If you snap one shot, I'll break that thing." That point blank aggression sent a quick signal to the crew that it was not going to be easy. They stopped instantly and tried to disarm their aggressor, even though he was not physically armed. They merely invoked their interpersonal and conflict resolution skills.

"Don't feel offended sir, as we told you earlier, we are journalists and our mission here might be beneficial to you and your community. We saw a woman who says her name is Mrs. Rita Silas and that she hails from Naminsa." Idiapa felt stung by those words.

"It is a lie. It is a pure lie. Who do you want to deceive, me? How can you claim you saw a woman presumed drowned and may have been eaten by sea animals? May be you saw her ghost because we were reliably informed that she…."

"You are right sir, but she didn't die. She was thought dead and actually abandoned but was picked up by some expatriate oil workers."

"Please wait, I am not going to hear this alone." He got up and went to gather his people. The crew, exchanging familiar looks and smiles, waited silently. Before they knew what was going on, seven men had come to join them. Mary looked at them and wondered where they kept all their women.

"What about her fellow women? Are they not around?" Mary inquired, attracting their attention.

"Please repeat what you said, gentleman," Idiapa addressed Clifford, pointedly ignoring Mary. But Mary, quite seasoned in male/female issues and very aware of the conditioning and socialisation problems that faced the society of the day, understood Idiapa and did not press further, especially as Idiapa was already worked up, right from the beginning. Clifford narrated his story once more and the pin drop silence that followed gave the impression that they had all suddenly been struck dumb. Elder James, an outspoken retired technocrat eventually spoke, posing a question to Clifford. Johnny resumed video filming and snapping with the still camera at intervals, this time, uninterrupted.

"My son, are you sure you saw our wife?"

"I saw a woman, a pregnant woman, who is named Mrs. Rita Silas…"

"Pregnant woman, did you say pregnant?" interrupted Idiapa, actually howling. Clifford nodded.

"My brothers, hear what he is saying. Was Rita ever pregnant after Biase? Are these people not a bunch of jokers? Don't people answer the same names, coincidentally? Are they talking about her or her daughter? I don't understand where these people are coming from."

"Easy Idiapa, the only way to find out is to go there," and turning to Clifford, Elder James asked, "Can you take us to see her?"

"Of course sir, at the opportune time at a later date you will definitely see her. We equally have news about her daughter but that will be for later. In the meantime, our investigation continues. We'll be taking our leave now. Thank you for your time."

"Go well" Idiapa wished them. And, lowering his voice, "with your lies."

The elders of Naminsa watched them leave and Elder James took a hard look at Idiapa and said to him

"Those are journalists either on national assignment or social development work. Why were you hostile to them?"

"Me, was I hostile to them? They were talking nonsense and I did not want them to continue. Does that amount to hostility? How can they say they saw a pregnant Rita and therefore she is Oyiga's wife? What business of theirs is it?"

"Idiapa, those people may be harbingers of good news. Please when next they come, treat them more humanely, you never can tell."

"Okay, I've heard you. Till they come"

Perplexed and unable to say anything more, the elders dispersed quietly one after another.

"Cliff, weren't you scared? I thought that the man was going to pounce on us." John spoke.

"Is he drunk? I was ready to stop him if he tried, Ah ah, such people are familiar nah. We know them" Cliff replied confidently.

"But the man hostile o, no be small. See how he ignored me when I asked about the women. He must be a very difficult person. It is amazing that in spite of all our development effort, such people still exist." Mary seemed not to be able to take Idiapa off her mind.

"If he had broken this camera, na hin be say work for end. But who go allow am touch the camera, me? That's where he missed it. I was very mindful." John added.

"Okay guys, finish your drinks and let's be on our way. It's been tough for us today." Clifford urged, knowing that they had had enough break. One more link established plus confirmation of an element of hostility, the CNN crew set out to produce reports on all links. Not exactly an issue, Idiapa's hostility was waved aside and, after a short period of consistent hard work, all major interviews were now completed and fine-tuned.

Strategically fitting all stories into deserving pages and corners in English and vernacular, Community News Magazine popped with the caption of the big story: "Dead Woman Found Alive, Pregnant." Looking quite catchy and paradoxical, this headline dwarfed all other stories and expectedly stirred up people's eagerness to know what the edition had to offer. Several copies were sold and in fact, long before the next edition was due, every single copy had been sold. Good news for CNN, aided by the magazine's wide reach, community outlook and interest. FRAP being a community based organisation (CBO) spared no effort in ensuring that grassroots needs and interests were covered.

The acceptability of the magazine was an eloquent testimony to the fact that the grassroots' strong need for community and other news had not been met. It was time to fill the gap and get the grassroots involved in reading stories about their surrounding and other areas. CNN was on ground to bridge this gap and address the issue, quite often, in collaboration with FRAP. The magazine coming in two parts - English and vernacular copies, was actually icing on the cake. This had become a regular feature. All CNN project proposals had a sure budget line for translating and transcribing scripts and stories into vernacular.

# CHAPTER ELEVEN

## Everywhere I go I see you

"Read and see for yourself," Doctor Stapyioth said, as he handed Rita a copy of the magazine. "The heavens may have smiled at us," he added as the woman's face sparkled with momentary delight. Stapyioth planted a steady gaze on her, with a heartfelt smile. Rita flipped through and read with mixed feelings, peering into the magazine, trying to study the pictures and ascertain that the images represented the true persons.

"No, no, this can't be Biase. It's her face alright, but how come she looks so bloated?"

Rita went into another bout of sobbing, concluding that her daughter must have contracted a terrible disease that left her bloated.

"Doctor, can one just get bloated like this for no reason? Has my daughter been struck by a strange disease?"

"Madam, life comes first. Initially, we did not know that she was alive. Now we know and you are working yourself up concerning her size. I thought we should look forward to seeing her and ascertaining her true size. What if she just added weight? Why are you trying to convert good news to sour news? Please wipe those tears and keep your fingers crossed."

"Okay, Doctor."

Doctor Stapyioth gave her another smile and left.

Suspecting everything but pregnancy, her gaze went to the picture of the community meeting between her husband's people and the crew; and strangely, she felt nostalgic and longed to return home. Before seeing the magazine, the television in her hospital room had earlier flashed the same story as a news item, and now she was looking at the same images again, further confirming those she had seen on television. She held on to the magazine, thinking of everything under the sun. Shortly after, she fell asleep.

At the Raboni's, Biase closed the book she was reading on seeing her friend step in with a spring. It was a book written by one of her favourite Nigerian authors. Sophie had come to confirm the veracity of the news making the rounds in Naminsa.

"Biase, did you hear the news about people going about interviewing people?" Sophie asked

Oh yes, my sister. The people came here to ask me questions. They told me that my mother is alive and well, can you imagine that? Isn't God wonderful? Hmm Sophie, come closer." When she did, Biase whispered into her ear "they told me that mum is pregnant." Then the excitement turned into tears that stood in her eyes as she added, "Mum was pregnant before the trip and she did not know it and people were jeering at her." The tears dropped like rainfall.

"Can't you see that at least we are getting somewhere? Stop crying, Biase. We are getting somewhere." Sophie used her bare palm to wipe the tears on her friend's face. She had not heard the bit about Biase's mother's pregnancy before her visit and so felt kind of scandalised at the situation whereby mother and unmarried daughter were pregnant at the same time.

"Hey! Biase, I can't get over the fact that both of you are pregnant at the same time."

"I am very uncomfortable about the situation, but it is beyond my control." Sophie was of the view that some other girls would long have found a solution to that problem, to avoid ugly situations in the future.

"What kind of solution?" Biase asked.

Sophie who was quite unprepared for that question, blurted out, wondering if she had not spoken unwittingly.

"No, it's nothing Biase. I had nothing in particular in mind. It's just that Naminsa will resume its hostility, this time a different brand. You know they don't mind their business in that community. How does that make you feel?" Biase's mood could not be described as bad. Sophie's visits always brought about a rather strange sour and sweet combination of feelings.

"I don't care anymore. I have developed a thick skin. I am just praying for safe delivery for my mum and me, and for the Almighty to prove to Naminsa that nothing is in their hands. Nothing at all – and that everything is controlled by the Omnipotent. Little wonder Michael W. Smith was very expressive when he sang – Everywhere I Go, I See You. I want the people of Naminsa to open their eyes so they can see Him as well and know that they cannot dictate to Him what He would do and when He would do it. I am so overwhelmed by the joy of my mother's pregnancy that I am not worried anymore about myself. At least now I know we neither converted fish into children nor children into fish. I can't wait to see Mum."

Sophie noticed the misty and red eyes when Biase turned to her and asked, "Did they say when she is expected back home?"

Watching Biase with admiration, Sophie whose eyes were equally misty shook her head slowly, drawing a deep breath.

"My plan is for none of those Naminsa busy bodies to see me pregnant. By God's grace, I'll have my baby here and if by that time, Mummy has come back, I'll be going to see her from here. You know the community people have a way of adopting one line of reasoning and becoming blind to others, so much so that they appear dumb in some of their actions. Most of them having not seen me pregnant will never know I carried a pregnancy and had a baby. Even if they are told, they will not believe it. To them, seeing, is believing. Only those who my uncle and his wife told will know and I can bet they kept sealed lips because of the embarrassment it would have caused them – you know, amidst news of my father's death and mother's disappearance. So, as far as they are concerned, I am just away from home. Some of them who have heard will want to wait and see, and when eventually they see me not pregnant and not with baby, they will simply justify their unbelief and let go. You get me?" Biase charged, paused to take a deep breath. She resumed, after Sophie had given her a solidarity nod.

"Hmm! Sophie, I was reading a book before you came in. I got the book from the library. You see, everything in that book, I totally agree with. Let me read some portions to you. Sophie, are you listening?" Sophie nodded.

"People like to pursue blindly this phenomenon called culture and they pursue it until they fall into a pit, without realising it. Blind pursuit of culture obviously is as repressive as it is counter-productive. It fuels underdevelopment. It is the bane of the developing world. Children are born into it and become socialised and conditioned into accepting and imbibing it as a way of life. People become resistant to change, allowing old and unproductive, sometimes harmful practices, habits, characters, utterances, behaviours, norms and customs to persist and hold sway. Do you not agree Sophie?"

"I agree. Everything you have just read out is true. No doubt," Sophie concurred.

Biase continued.

"Just try to liken what I have just read, to our community. Naminsa tacitly pushes childless couples to suicidal levels and that is called culture. And if the couple happens to have only daughters or one daughter, they tease the couple and tag them 'those who wash their hands clean only to use the washed hands to crack kernel for the chicken.' And if the couple has only one boy, they describe the couple as 'carrying earthenware pot on the head.' For with only one stumble, the clay pot may drop on the ground. Is that not what we hear them say all the time?"`

"Yes, all the time, Biase. With just one stumble, the pot drops and breaks into pieces."

Sophie nodded.

"The author goes ahead to say, just listen: 'One bad thing about culture is that it gives the people a wrong notion of doing the right thing even when it is detrimental to their psyche, their health, marriages, education, economy and other areas. Most times, it is shrouded in ignorance and passed down the generations as inheritance, hence you hear them say that their forefathers did it and so they must do it. Yet there are many things their forefathers did not do which they are doing. Who knows, the forefathers might be frowning from where they are now, at people traveling by air and using the Internet. It is shameful that in this modern, jet age and age of the computer, people are still clinging on to undignifying and unedifying cultures, customs and traditions. There is so much dirt in the scrotum and we are busy washing our feet with the little soap available." Sophie chuckled, as Biase finished reading that portion.

"Hey Biase, you are talking so much sense oh. I must read that book. I could continue listening to you but I must get going now so as to avoid sunset. When next I come, we'll continue". She chuckled again, gripped by the humour she found in the bit about the scrotum. But unsmiling, Biase was not done yet.

"Sorry Sophie, I did not realise that we've gone this far into the day but not to worry, you'll get home before sunset. The bike men are always there waiting for passengers. You see, Sophie, we are talking about the problems that await us and generations coming after us. If we don't start, and continue to talk about them, they might just remain unsolved problems that would continue affecting us. We must not allow it; we must start doing something, no matter how small, and the time to begin is now."

"I agree with that writer. The perception, behaviour and approach of our people in Naminsa must change..." Sophie concluded.

"Hey baby, give me five."

They got up and slammed their right palms together in unbridled solidarity.

"We are right on!" Sophie topped up, heading for the exit and wishing Biase well.

# CHAPTER TWELVE

## The Big Apology

Rita's twins came a bit prematurely but the babies and their mother were in a stable condition. Stapyioth who was worried stiff about the early arrival of the babies heaved a sigh of relief when all tests on the babies showed strong reflexes – stronger than those in some babies born at full term. He was already considering making arrangements to hire or fly in incubators since their health facility was not equipped with any, probably because the clinic was set up as a centre to cater for the immediate ailments of their on-and-off-shore personnel. Rita Silas was just a test case of their recent community response policy. Stapyioth had initially planned to invite a surgeon who would perform a Caesarean section on Rita but the babies appeared bent on coming out unaided. Two lovely male babies, slowly kicking and punching at exactly nobody! One of them was already sticking his tiny finger into his mouth.

"Oh my God! Never in my several years of practice have I experienced such awesomeness!" Stapyioth's body was covered in goose pumps. "God is indeed awesome." The babies were truly cute and Stapyioth, proud of their efforts and achievement as far as mother and babies were concerned, pampered them with healthcare and love. Such attention came not only from Stapyioth, but from all the health workers and people of the neighbourhood.

The doctor advised Rita to put the babies to the breast as soon as possible and let them draw out the colostrum into their tiny system, for protection, before the milk proper began to flow. A few days after delivery, gifts trickled in for the babies and Rita was overwhelmed at the show of love and goodwill. She breastfed her babies exclusively and would have been completely sapped, were it not for the good nutrition the clinic provided, through the balanced diet they always fed her. It was a huge relief when she introduced the formula milk to complement breast milk.

The pile up of cartons of formula milk in one corner of the hospital room indicated that the hospital authorities would support her for much longer. The twins and their mother looked so healthy that Dr. Stapyioth and the hospital management had begun to discuss the procedure for their return to their home.

"I wonder why those impostors have not come back with more information as promised," Idiapa spoke first.

"Idiapa, I hope it is not those journalists you are calling impostors? I think the group came with a purpose and knew what they were doing," one elder remarked.

"Alright, let them come and conclude their tale of how they saw a pregnant Rita. Rita, the woman who managed to give us a child, just one girl and then turned male herself. Can a man be pregnant?"

"Idiapa, show some undersanding," the elder admonished.

"And respect too," another also warned.

"People cannot just walk into a community and begin to say what they do not know about. Those people came with a purpose," the first elder reiterated.

"What purpose? What...?" One elder looked at him and shook his head. Elder Josomo walked in briskly and attracted everybody's attention, interrupting Idiapa and the other kinsmen who were meeting again to deliberate on the issues concerning Rita and her daughter, Biase. Elder Josomo, clutching a copy of the community news magazine published by CNN, sat down, all ears. He began to fan himself with the magazine, expecting to join in the discussion. Idiapa sat down too. Then Josomo spoke.

"I knew that those journalists were gathering their facts and putting them together. That is probably why they have not come back to us, and perhaps too, because we were not exactly friendly to them." And shifting his attention to Idiapa said, "Maybe you should have been a bit nicer to them, for record purposes and for posterity." He pointed momentarily at Idiapa. And holding up the magazine he came with, before Idiapa who glared at him could respond, he said, "See the magazine they have produced. My son returned from the city yesterday with this copy and brought the information in it to my attention. See, her picture is right here and on the next page is her daughter's."

"Give me that paper!" The force and irritation in Idiapa's voice did not surprise the elders.

"No, Josomo bring it here!"

"I should be the one handling that paper. Is it not all about my brother's family?" Idiapa protested.

Elder Omadi was the one who got hold of the magazine and, staring into the pages, began to flip through. The other elders came around to catch a glimpse. Together, peering and trying to hold the magazine, they almost tore it. The initial scramble was now over and the men took their turn to study the publication. The stories and interviews were all there. The documented format had arrested them. Minutes passed before Idiapa summoned the courage to speak.

"Oh dear, I feel very disturbed by these pictures Josomo has just showed us. Hei, my brother died without knowing that his wife was carrying their long-awaited pregnancy. We did not even know that the woman was alive. Please my brothers, how can we get the woman back home? That is my major concern now. I implore you to assist me, please, brothers."

Josomo stirred in his seat.

"Idiapa, why are you this hard? In fact, I will call a spade a spade. Idiapa, why are you this wicked? If you open that your stupid mouth and voice an apology, what would happen to you? You owe your brother, his wife, daughter and us a huge apology. You will start by admitting that you have done wrong and go ahead to beg us to forgive you; otherwise we'll deal with you the community way and...."

"Elders, can you hear Josomo?"

"We can. He is right! No one losses his manhood if he says the truth. Jesomo is right. Your recalcitrance is unbearable. We are tired. You have attacked everybody, your brother, his wife and daughter, the journalists and even your fellow elders. Ah, ah? You are indeed an attacker, at your age!"

"Now it is our turn to attack you. Those wings of yours need to be clipped."

The elders looked at Idiapa, expecting his apology. He had his face down. They wondered if it was out of shame or remorse. Or was he being adamant? Almost one minute passed and Idiapa did not say anything. Elder Josomo got up.

"Fellow elders, as far as I am concerned, this meeting is over. I am leaving."

"Same here", said another.

Yet another elder got up, and another. As they moved away from the meeting venue, Idiapa sprang up and ran after them. He went past them and was now facing them.

"Fellow elders please don't do this to me. I know what you mean. I understand but, but… Please come back, I'll make it up. Come back please."

The elders looked at one another, and with gesticulations, agreed to go back. Now seated once more, Idiapa stood before them.

"Fellow elders, I am so very sorry. I know I have wronged everyone. Sometimes I feel that if I had not put undue pressure on my brother, he might be alive today. Please forgive me. I am aware that if I cook for the community, the food will be exhausted but if the community cooks for me, I cannot finish the food. The community comes first before me. Forgive me, my brothers. I wish my brother can forgive me wherever he is now. In due course, I shall apologise to his widow and daughter. I also…"

"That's okay, Idiapa; we have heard you. But as we all know, apology calms the mind but does not save spilt milk. Idiapa, the milk has already been spilled. Do you know how to reach your late brother's wife?"

Idiapa shook his head.

"And you want us to accompany you there. So how do we get there?" Josomo paused as if expecting an answer from an already broken Idiapa. "Look", he continued, "it is all in the magazine, the hospital where she is on admission, its address and even the direction on how to get there. The name of the medical director and other information are here. It says here that the woman is due to have her baby soon. Do you know whether she has had her baby or not?"

Idiapa shook his head again.

"And you did not want the magazine and its journalists. You were harsh to them, the independent investigators. You should be ashamed of yourself. In fact, I am ashamed of you. You are so ignorant of current issues and stupidly full of yourself. See the mess you have single-handedly thrown the community into. I don't even know how to start handling you." Josomo took a breather, and as if calming himself, added, "Anyway, this is no time to dilly dally." He paused and looked at them all one by one, as if to draw more inspiration from their acquiescence. "This is time to drop your meanness. Idiapa, I am directing this at you again. You think that life is all about fighting. Remember how you almost attacked the 'good Samaritans' who came to seek information from us? I mean the journalists. You went for their camera and they had to pack up and leave before you could do any damage to them and their equipment. Our pictures would have been in this magazine but you spoilt everything. Now only the short interview which they managed to get is documented. What have you gained? What have you achieved? You do not achieve anything with negative attitude."

"Yes, Josomo, now he wants us to accompany him. Wouldn't it have been nice to have our pictures in this paper for all to see?" The furious elder who was waving the magazine at Idiapa gave his last shot. "Mr. Too know," he added and sat down. Idiapa was still looking downwards.

There was silence. Elder Josomo planted a gaze on Idiapa, shaking his head slowly with a hiss of disappointment. Then he admonished, "Idiapa, sometimes I find it difficult to understand you; you fail to act when you are expected to. I was listening to hear you say you want to go tomorrow to seek out your brother's wife and probably bring her home but here you are asking, 'how can we get the woman back home?' You know how and I think it is by going there tomorrow, not day after tomorrow, but tomorrow. Elders, do I speak your mind?" he asked, casting quick glances at them.

"You speak our mind, Josomo," they chorused, and one of them asked about the woman's daughter.

"Her picture is also in the magazine, just her face," Josomo was quick to reply. "The news in the magazine has it that the girl is a resident at that Home in the neighbouring town where they look after helpless people," Josomo said, as he pointed towards the direction of the Raboni's, "and I was going to ask Idiapa if his late brother's daughter has become helpless, and why?" Idiapa's eyes were fixed to the ground as if counting the tiny stones of the sand.

"Yes," another elder cut in. "It is a shameful act, Idiapa, if it is true that your brother's only daughter resides in a Home for the helpless when you have a home and a wife. It is an abominable act. You owe the community an explanation, if it is true o, because I find it hard to believe."

"Yes. We must tackle that when we finish with this one we are faced with now. What a disgrace! If you could not cater for her, why didn't you bring her to me? My wife would have cared for her in the absence of her father, your brother, and her mother," another added.

Idiapa was piqued but could not speak. He swallowed hard, breathing fast. They reminded him that it was not a usual occurrence in the traditional African extended family system for a young girl to be left to her fate that way.

"Even your wife allowed that to happen? What kind of a couple are you? Is it because your own daughter is married and your other children are boys? This matter is too serious to be postponed. He must be fined."

Idiapa searched in vain for where to hide his face. He moped in silence. He raised his head and began to speak to his kinsmen, thanking them for their time and concern, returning gratitude to elder Josomo for his useful tips, which he had heeded, and requesting them to accompany him to the creeks the next day.

"Where is your brother's daughter, Idiapa?" Elder Omadi asked, not allowing Idiapa to brush that aside. "She is equally important to us. Don't evade the question. Where is she? Tell us before we move ahead."

"Please, elders, I beg you again. I know I have erred, I have already admitted my guilt. I ask you to forgive me and my wife. We wronged that girl and I feel terrible about it but you must not throw away the bath water with the baby still in it. I will get her back here as soon as possible. It's a promise."

The angered silence that followed had a way of speaking to the situation and the elders understood that they could shift grounds a little, just a bit. So they decided to give him a fine of one goat and four thousand naira, instead of five thousand naira. Idiapa appreciated the elder's leniency and promptly paid up after the meeting. He was lucky not to have been ostracized, considering the enormity of his offence.

## CHAPTER THIRTEEN

# The Big Surprise

The elders decided that two volunteers would accompany Idiapa on a fact-finding trip. Idiapa was to foot the bill and he was willing to do so but was a bit scared of the unknown.

"Oh God, please help me out of this one and I will praise you forever," he prayed, as he thought about everything that had transpired. Elders Taruma and Jini showed up on time and the trio set out. The journey was quite ordinary until they got to the point where they had to use the speed boat and emotions began to whip up.

"This was what killed my brother," Idiapa began, pointing at the water.

"I just hope we shall be safe."

"The boats don't capsize every day, do they? And even if they do, must they target only people from Naminsa?" Jini asked, expecting answers from no one in particular.

"It is not our lot. We shall get to that hospital and come back via the speed boat and nothing, absolutely nothing will go wrong." Taruma said, adding, "We should all learn to swim."

"How and when? At this age, it is too late. Perhaps you mean we should have learnt to swim in the water wells that have served as our source of water? Is that what you mean, Taruma?"

"Taruma, you are lucky to have learned to swim when as a young man you lived outside the community, serving someone. Isn't it?" Idiapa asked and Taruma nodded.

"Don't forget the story told by elders that in the olden days, the king's only son drowned trying to swim while on an expedition to another land with his friends. The community elders were so grieved at the death of the royal heir that they placed an embargo on swimming. This has been passed down the generations. I am not sure how much water it holds now. What I am sure about is that we shall go and come back. But it is good to learn to swim so as to be able to avoid the type of calamity that befell our brother Oyiga. Let's go!" Jini concluded.

At Shores Clinic 2, Dr. Stapyioth was on hand to receive them even though it was an impromptu visit. He took down their names and went to the hospital room to inform Rita about the visit and confirmed that they were indeed her people, before taking them to see her. The three men were stunned at what they saw - a more beautiful but unenthusiastic Rita, with two cribs by her side. They shivered like people who had caught the fever and could not talk. One of them had his eyes wide open with his lower lip drooping. They however managed to bend slightly to give her a hug each, in her sitting position.

"I greet you, elders of the land," Rita welcomed them.

"We greet you too, our dear wife," Idiapa responded for the team. The other elders followed suit and that served as the curtain raiser, with Rita wondering for a second when she became a 'dear wife' to Idiapa, who spoke again.

"We read about everything in the magazine," sighting a copy on her hospital locker, "oh, you too have a copy,"

Rita nodded.

"You've already had the baby; we didn't know," and seeing that Rita and two babies were the only occupants of the room, wanted Rita to clear the air. "So which of these babies is ours?" At this point, Stapyioth who had been watching the mild drama intoned.

"Mrs. Silas is the proud mother of a set of male twins. We are happy to have delivered her of the boys. We thank God."

"Eh! Male twins?" The men chorused.

"Yes, male twins and as you can see, both mother and babies are doing well. The woman had a very tough time but thank Goodness, she came through strongly. She is very fortunate."

The men stood speechless, just looking at each other, while Rita remained pensive. Stapyioth only just realised that his guests had not been offered seats. He promptly withdrew and seconds later, attendants came in with chairs for them. Minutes after the chairs had been made available, the men could still not sit down and Rita probably was still too dazed to get into conversation with them, or was simply trying to ignore them for a while. Dr. Stapyioth came back and, finding them still standing, said, pulling the chairs closer to them, "Gentlemen, please sit down. The chairs are for you. Make yourselves comfortable." At this point Idiapa asked his kinsmen to sit down, and it was only then that he could summon courage to sit himself. He spoke further to Rita.

"You had twins, two boys? Jesus of Nazareth!" He had his arms folded across his chest. "Hm hm! We thank God for your life. Please forget the past, I beg you and let's together look up to a better future", he said, stirring up Rita's already swelling emotion. He stood up, walked up to the cribs, peered into them and said "Twins! Oh, thank God." He raised open palms up. "But how come, Rita; you were not aware that you..., did you know that you were..., I mean, how did..., was my brother aware? I mean, I thank God, I just thank God. I am very happy and the only thing I can do now is to place you all in God's care"

Rita issued a wry smile and nodded, and one of the elders said to her, "Our wife, we were so happy to learn that you are alive. We thank those magazine people who brought everything to light. Then your brother-in-law asked us to come with him. We were not expecting to see you with these lovely twins. Two boys! But we are excited about them and thank God Almighty. God has done wonders and we are grateful to Him. Congratulations, our dear wife!"

"Thank you, elder."

"See how they both look like Oyiga. Oh dear Oyiga, chai."

Idiapa nodded vigorously. He stood akimbo for a while. Then he turned back to Rita and asked: "So when should we come to take you home?"

"Take me home to where? Do I have a home?" Rita snapped back.

"My brother's wife, please, I beg you. I am very sorry. If I were to have another opportunity, I would not repeat this mistake. Forgive me."

Rita took a deep breath and heaved a sigh.

"Our wife, please do not talk this way. We know how hurt you are. You should be; you are human but remember that to err is human and to forgive is divine. Please forgive and forget. In fact we plead with you to forgive the entire community." Elder Fini's passionate plea seemed to have made more meaning to Rita.

"The hospital authorities will decide when I will leave here. I think you should ask the doctor," Rita demurred.

Idiapa located Dr. Stapyioth in his office and he unfolded the hospital management's plan for the woman to Idiapa, who was dazed at the largesse announced. Stapyioth also told Idiapa how they would go about it, and that very soon Rita and her babies would be home. Still dazed, Idiapa thanked Stapyioth and returned to his kinsmen in the hospital room. Soon after, they bade Rita bye and left. Idiapa disclosed Stapyioth's plan to the two men who accompanied them and wondered if the hospital will allow him handle part of the hospital's plan, as the representative of Rita's late husband. He voiced his desire and the two other men read his lips immediately. He was, true to type, already thinking of what he could make from the whole exercise. They had expected to see a quiet and penitent man all through the journey back to Naminsa; failing which, they just could not spare him.

"There you go again, Idiapa. Don't you have shame? In spite of all your atrocities, you want to be the one to handle the hospital's plan for Rita, her sons and daughter. You are already wondering if... I salute your courage but if I were you, I would steer clear and wait to be invited. Please show that you have some dignity."

Taken aback, Idiapa looked at Taruma, trying to complain with his eyes.

"Fini is telling you what should obtain," Taruma also hit him with what they both considered to be the truth. "Yes, we know that you are the male elder in the compound but in the prevailing circumstances, I advise that you hold yourself. Show more remorse. I thought you would have wondered how to connect with Rita's daughter first. Idiapa, please." Taruma said to him, raising an open palm to his face.

Back home, the community went agog with the news of Rita and the twins. Idiapa had called a meeting to give them the good news. The women went into their usual child birth dance jumping higher for the birth of a male, and more fiercely for male twins.

One week after the visit of the Naminsa three, the Stapyioth team paid their preliminary visit to Naminsa, to assess the amount of work to be done there before Rita's return. Naminsa was hundreds of miles from the creeks where the oil firms were located but the Stapyioth team meant business and were bent on completing what they started. When they picked up Rita, they neither knew who she was nor where she came from. They were out to prove a point and ofcourse Rita was exceptionally lucky, having not come from the creeks? Could it be providence working? Why did things happen the way they did? Will Naminsa and others learn from all this? The Shores 2 team returned to work, and based on Stapyioth's report and recommendation, the authorities decided to refurbish Oyiga's house. Within that same week, another group, apparently of professional contractors were in Naminsa to inspect the building and ascertain how much work to be done. Naminsa had never seen anything like that before. Each time a group came for inspection, the community gathered to watch. The contractors hired some local Naminsa handlers to be part of the work team. Idiapa had perhaps taken the advice of Taruma and Fini, and had tried to comport himself with some prestige, and it paid off. The contractor got him to act as the supervisor.

"My oh my! What a new look, the house is now wearing! What a bright colour of paint! Hmm, it makes it stand out, and us too. I am glad to be part of the work team, thanks Idiapa," Taruma said with excitement and before Idiapa could respond, Pini intoned.

"Apart from the outward look, the fine interior décor is singing a sweet tune, melodious indeed. Thanks, Idiapa, for including our names."

"That's okay. I am glad you advised me on the way to go. Thank you too."

Oyiga's house attracted admirers and onlookers, and Idiapa somehow felt proud on behalf of his late brother, wondering if indeed this new phenomenon was real. At the hospital, the authorities had stored up everything that was to be taken to Naminsa for Rita and the babies, in readiness for the trip, but Dr. Stapyioth had been concerned about the health security of their precious twins. He had once wondered aloud how the babies would access primary healthcare, and had actually tried to find out from Rita.

"There is no Primary Health institution in Naminsa. You are referring to Community Health Centre, isn't it?" Stapyioth nodded and Rita gave out a sad sigh. "The people have to go far to get their babies immunised. It is hard for them and because of that; most times they do not bother to go."

"You mean that because of the difficulty in accessing healthcare, the people do not bother to go distances?" Stapyioth sought clarification, his face glowed.

"Yes doctor. They resort to traditional healthcare methods."

"That's quite scary. I just fear that there could be a considerable level of infant mortality in Naminsa, including maternal mortality."

"Naminsa needs a good health centre where everybody can go for medical treatment when ill." Rita was emphatic. Stapyioth was thinking deeper than his nods revealed. He indeed feared for the safety of 'his babies' and did not want to take chances. He began to chip it in and make far-reaching suggestions in management meetings preceding the take-off to Naminsa. But another hospital official in one of those meetings thought otherwise.

"Yes, our aim is to see our host communities comfortable and happy and we shall ensure that. As for the twins, I am thinking that providing the community with a borehole water source would be more appropriate as water is life and at least, they have a distant hospital to go to. More so, as your report stated that they use water wells."

"Better still," Stapyioth suggested. "We can give them both, we can actually afford both and in any case, it helps our image as we shall involve that NGO and their news magazine, for publicity, and this could go far. What do you think?"

"Great idea but my worry is that two major projects for one community could be counter-productive. There are other communities that equally need help. A health centre would require equipment and personnel, including continuous provision of drugs and oversight functions. We might not be exactly prepared to handle all that. At best, we could partner with government in this regard at a later date. Or better still, can we start with a borehole?" Some other person suggested.

"I think you are right, Dr. Freeman. Borehole first," Dr. Stapyioth concluded. Everybody concurred and one central community borehole was added to the list of deliverables for Naminsa. This was to take place later, after Rita and the twins would have settled down in their new home.

# CHAPTER FOURTEEN

## The EDD

Biase strolled around the premises of the Raboni medical center. Not even her cute maternity apparel provided by the Sisters could rob her of her sheer innocence, which elicited both admiration and sympathy. Her pregnancy had come to full term and she was just waiting for her due moment. The expected delivery date (EDD) had slipped by uneventfully and Biase continued going about her business. The Reverend Sisters had already put everything in place in anticipation of the baby's arrival. Sister Konsolina had accompanied her to the medical centre just a short walk away, where she was examined and found to still have some hours to go. On advice, she paced about the compound. When the cramps came, she bit her lower lip, uttered muffled cries and took in puffs of air. The nurses watched her closely and also timed her; and at a particular time, they called her in for another examination. Sister Konsolina, knowing that she had left Biase in capable hands, went back to the Home.

"Alright now, you just remain here and continue with the breathing exercise, you are doing very well; keep it up."

Biase nodded.

"If you continue this way, we'll be done in no time," the midwife Reverend Sister assured her. As the intermittent pain came and she groaned, her eyeballs bulged. She panted, moving her head from side to side, sometimes closing her eyes tightly because of pain. When the pain became unbearable, she cried out in full tears and screams, and this attracted the midwife's attention. After a quick re-examination, the midwife asked her to push when next the pain came. The pain came again and Biase gave a long push with all her strength and cry but the baby did not come out. She was tired already, fine beads of sweat dotting her forehead, her eyes dimming slightly. Her chest visibly moved up and down.

"You are doing well, Biase; we just need a little more push and your baby will be out, okay?" The midwife never stopped encouraging her.

"Okay!" Biase muttered, overwhelmed by pain. She was panting and *hmm, hmm, hmm* could be heard clearly. The sheer words of encouragement from the midwife seemed to have gingered the travailing teenager who let out a progression of strong youthful groans and pushes; and the head of the baby crowned.

"Good, my darling; you are so sweet. Just give me one more push. Just one more and we're there."

Biase, feeling as if the midwife's words came straight from heaven, firmly grabbed the edges of the couch, locked her lips and eyes in a tight clench, and pushed with all the strength remaining in her. And suddenly she felt a slippery fleshy substance slide through her cervix. The midwife's gloved hands caught the baby. Biase's baby cried heartily.

"That's it. Our baby is here. Good girl, Biase! Good girl! Congratulations! It's a boy!"

That did not mean anything to Biase, who was happy to be done with the exercise. She was startled when the midwife paused, stared at her and declared.

"There is one more."

"Hmm, one more what please?" Biase did not understand her.

"You have one more baby in your womb, another baby to be born; just a little more pushing to do."

"Haa, God have mercy, two?!"

"Yes two, my dear girl." She received a gentle pat on the shoulder from the midwife, who allowed a few more minutes to elapse.

"Let's go, no need to be scared. This will be easier. Come on, baby, Push!"

Biase had not undergone any scan prior to full term and so had no idea she was carrying twins. Another urge to push came but this time, her strong push was not as strenuous as the previous ones. The second boy slid into the waiting hands of the midwife, almost effortlessly.

"Congratulations, Biase!" And placing the babies on her chest, one after the other, she said, "You have two lovely male babies."

Biase moped, too tired to respond, and gave the midwife something between a smile and a grin, looked at her babies again and held them with both arms. She closed her eyes tightly and tears streamed. The midwife looked at Biase shook her head gently in love, wondering what Biase's fresh tears could be for. Were they tears of joy, pain or regret? She lifted the babies one after the other and placed one each in the two cribs just by the bedside. She was still watching Biase who, still breathing heavily, went into deep sleep, as if sedated. She woke up to find Sophie by her bedside. Sophie noticed that her friend's face looked fuller, fresher and more succulent. She looked around and thought she could smell a combination of blood, drugs and disinfectant. Her nose twitched, her eyes went from corner to corner and she observed that Biase was the lone occupant of the 10-bed ward. As Sophie waited, she flipped through an illustrated bible story book she found on a bedside locker. Biase had her twins between the hours of five and six in the morning and had fallen asleep thereafter. Sophie had spent precisely thirty minutes before Biase stirred, opened her eyes slightly and slept off again. She became totally awake at 11 am, when she dragged a yawn and faintly uttered some words in the hearing of Sophie.

"I am very hungry. I need to eat something. Please get me something to eat."

Sophie sprang to her feet and ran to the nurses' station. They had anticipated the situation and were indeed ready for Biase's demand. She sat up slowly and, within minutes, had finished eating a serving of bean pudding and hot corn pap with milk and sugar. She asked for more pap. After eating up everything, she remained silent for a while, head bowed, breathing deep. Then she raised her head and talked to her friend.

"Thank you, Sophie," Biase picked her words.

A glimpse at Biase in such deep slumber when Sophie came in made her almost conclude that something strange had happened to her friend. She could therefore not allow Biase to say one more word before she took over the talking.

"Thank God, Biase. You had a safe delivery. You must have gone through a difficult process, hmm? You Biase, now a mother," she wondered aloud, pointing her index finger at Biase, and asking further, "What happened, how did it go?"

"Sophie my sister, it is better experienced than explained. I have never felt so much pain in my life. Now can you imagine my surprise when the midwife told me there was one more baby?"

"One more baby, where?"

"In my belly."

"Twins?"

"Yes Sophie, twins!"

"Ehn? Oh my God! How did it happen?"

"I don't know Sophie. Just join me in thanking God. It was hectic. The pain was too much. Even as I talk to you, I have serious cramps below my belly and the stitches I received are hurting."

"Stitches," Sophie repeated, wondering.

"Yes, I had some cuts that made for an easier passage for the babies. After delivery, they had to stitch up." Biase explained, still weak, while Sophie cringed. All covered in goose bumps, she closed her eyes tightly, either in pain or fright, apparently realising that the fowl watching the killing of the chicken might be witnessing, so to speak, its own killing method, invariably. Sophie felt very sorry for Biase and looked at her with tender affection.

"Where are the babies?"

"In the Nursery"

"Hmm!" Sophie was amazed.

Seeing that her friend looked tired and drowsy even after just waking up from sleep, Sophie sensed that Biase needed some quiet and decided to leave and come back the next day.

"Biase please go back to sleep. I'll come again tomorrow. Remember that I am here to assist in any way you need me to."

"Thank you, Sophie."

Sophie returned to the community and maintained sealed lips mostly because she was still dazed due to what she saw and felt at the clinic. She lay on the bed, slowly taking in the aura and complexity of what she imagined her short stay with Biase represented. Sophie herself did not know what was wrong with her but her mother understood everything her daughter was going through, after Sophie managed to respond to her mother's searching questions.

"I went to see Biase, and mummy, do you know what?"

"What?" her mother snapped, torn between surprise and curiosity.

"Biase had safe delivery of her babies."

"Eh? What did you just say? Did you say babies?"

"Yes, mum. She also had twins."

"Okokobioko! Sophie, stop that joke now." She had her hands on her head.

"Mother, I am not joking. Biase was delivered of a set of bouncing twin babies, both male. The babies were in the Nursery."

"God eh, hey, which kind one be this o? Another set of twins? I fear o." Sophie's mother was shivering from astonishment but when she remembered that it was her duty to calm her daughter rather than leave her further confounded; she drew Sophie close to her and began to rub her back.

"Sophie, life is like a journey on a road with bends and curves. No one knows when they'll get to a bend and where a curve is. Your friend is in a curve now but the road will straighten out afterwards, so shake off that feeling of gloom and relax. You see, as I have always told you, the French say 'ça passera', it will pass and everything will become normal again, someday. It's only a matter of time."

"She said they stitched her. Mum, is it with a needle?"

"Surgical needle. Small pain. Don't let all that bother you. It's all part of being a woman. It will be okay. When are you seeing her again?"

"Tomorrow, mum. Infact, every day, I feel for her."

"Send my regards to her. I'll see her later."

"Okay, mum." Sophie's entire system had been overturned.

"If you are feeling this way, how would your friend feel? I have told you it is all part of being a woman and that within days; she would begin to come back to her old self. Relax girl, it is a good thing."

"Okay, mum," Sophie smiled broadly, making her mother more comfortable. Sophie looked forward to hearing more from Biase.

Days later, the Raboni Home was to have an expanded meeting, with Reverend Mother Anthonia and Reverend Fr. Lazarus in attendance. Fr. Lazarus was the priest in charge of the city center parish. He had an oversight function on the Home while Mother Anthonia was the Mother Superior of the Raboni Home.

"In the name of the Father…" Reverend Fr. Lazarus began. And they all made the sign of the cross.

"And of the Son, and of the Holy Spirit, Amen, they chorused."

And he said a prayer, after which the meeting began.

"Sisters, I hope it is no crime if I start with tea?" Fr. Laz was already walking toward the tea stand. "I am starving." The others followed suit and it became a relaxed tea/coffee meeting.

"I called this meeting to discuss the plight of the young girl, Biase, who has been in our care for months now. She really needs to be further mentored as she has seen and suffered more than is necessary for her age." Mother Anthonia called the first shot.

"How old is she? I must have forgotten that," Fr. Laz asked.

"Seventeen"

"Oh yes, poor girl! I remember. Seventeen, homeless and with a set of twins; what a world"

"Not just that", Mother Theresa explained further. "Please look at the proper picture. A female sixteen-year-old only child running away with her parents to avoid rejection, she became victim of a boat mishap in which her father died and her mother missing but she was rescued. Her rescuer took her to his home to give her shelter for the night and later raped her. The rescuer's people, ignorantly suspicious of her, sent her away, back to her home community. That was rejection, a second time. The unfortunate rape had resulted in pregnancy and the girl's uncle, with his wife's connivance, sent her packing, making her face yet another rejection. Humanitarians doing God's work catered for her and saw her through pregnancy and the safe delivery of not one baby but twins at age seventeen. What do you do with such a girl? She can't just be sent away like that. We have to help her further. I am sure she took part in the classes running at the Home." The Sisters nodded.

"But more importantly, we should indeed worry about the inhumanity and impunity that abound in today's society. We must tackle these in any way we can, through the pulpits, newsletters, lectures, seminars and meetings. The church through the Home can assist this teenager further with her studies and perhaps see to the best form of care and survival for the babies. Sisters, it's now over to you. Counsel her and get her to understand the intricacies inherent in her situation and allow her to make her own choice."

"Thank you Fr. Laz. All hands are already on deck. We simply needed this extra encouragement from you. Right, Sisters?" Konsolina chipped in, turning to look at the other sisters.

"Yes Fr. Laz, sister Konso is right. All hands are truly on deck. Thank you very much, Fr." The others chorused.

"On behalf of Mother and all of us, I want to thank you sincerely for always coming around to boost our morale. You make us work harder because you give us the impression that we are already working hard. Thank you, Fr. Laz. I think lunch is already served. Sister Callista is already smiling across the table."

"Lunch, the tea and snacks have not quite digested but I can't refuse food from God's angels on earth. Thank you, ladies. Keep up the good works."

# CHAPTER FIFTEEN

## *Let Go*

Sophie went early to see Biase the next day so they could be together for much longer and have more time to exhaust their gist. They talked about a lot of issues – Naminsa, the Community News magazine, Biase's mother, and Biase herself. She told her friend that the latest news in Naminsa was about the awaited return of her mother from the riverine area. She told Biase that everything about her father's house looked new due to the touch-up, arranged by the oil company authorities.

"Our people are saying that it is misfortune turned blessing. Both the inside and outside of your home is now glittering and I hear that in the next couple of days, she will return". Biase was all ears. Sophie was a good friend indeed.

When she left, Reverend Sisters emerged from the staff area, gathered around Biase and engaged her in small talks. One of them spoke.

"Biase dear, this is not the end of your life. `In fact, it should be the beginning of a new dawn for you. It was a good move that you enrolled in both the spiritual and academic classes of the Raboni's. Your education is paramount. No one's cruelty to a woman should ever result in the end of the woman's ambition, dreams and aspiration. It might destabilise the plan for a while, but it should only be for a while. You must strive not to make it any longer than just a while, okay?"

Eyes already misty, Biase nodded and the counsellor said to her, "Biase, you have a whole bright future ahead, the ball is in your court. Rise up and take the bull by the horns."

Biase nodded again.

"You've been here for close to one year now and have become a mother. How do you intend to cope with your twins? Would you like to go back to Naminsa with your babies or send them to their biological father's home?

"No, no, neither. Their biological father's home is definitely out of the question. As for Naminsa, I just don't want to return there with the babies. My father is dead and I don't understand the story I am being told about my mother. My uncle and his wife loathed the sight of me so much; they threw me out of their house when they noticed I was..." Biase burst into tears and at this point the nurse drew her into a tight hug, urging her to put everything behind her and look forward. With bare hands, the nurse Reverend Sister wiped Biase's tears.

"They did not want to listen to my explanation. I had just lost my father and did not know where my mother was and my uncle and his wife pushed me out of their shelter and made me homeless." More sobs gripped her.

"But you have a home here or were you not taken care of at the Raboni's." Biase felt blackmailed as well as had her conscience prick her. Were her attitude and utterances devoid of gratitude? She wondered, and gave the counsellor a smile.

"Of course I was very well cared for. I appreciate it all. I am indeed very grateful and can never forget the goodness that emanated from the Raboni's. Thank you Sister." Biase said sincerely. The counsellor returned her smile.

"You must learn to begin to cast away that pathetic look of dejection you wear sometimes and replace it with a survivor's look of hope and optimism. You are a survivor and have showed that your bravery is not in doubt. All you need to do now is adorn that courage with confidence and you will unleash your full potential. It's all in you my dear, sweet girl."

Biase cried aloud. It was the ginger cry. The sister curdled Biase like a baby.

"We are trying to prepare you for what is ahead. We figure that in your complex situation, putting these babies up for adoption is quite a good option for you. It would be perhaps better than sending them to your home, Naminsa or to Pionto, their biological father's home or worse still, saddling you, a seventeen-year-old girl with the task of rearing a set of fatherless twins, at the expense of your academic pursuit. We are looking at the best for you."

Biase felt stung by a bee. "Hei, my babies!" A chilly string ran from her head to toes, causing her skin to be covered in goose bumps. Then fear overtook her and her body quaked. "Will I ever see them again? Will I see the adoptive parents? Will I know the whereabouts of my babies? Can't they remain here?" Sister was shaking her head to all the questions being posed by Biase.

"Biase, you need to know that custody of the babies will only be granted to foster parents who have the desire and means to take good care of them. But we give you the chance to make your own choice. We will respect your choice. Sorry, they can't remain here. We do not run a home for the motherless. We strive to prevent abortion and post abortion challenges in innocent victims. Thereafter, we offer the best solution and allow for choices to be made. Is that clear, Biase?"

"It is clear, Sister. Thanks a lot."

Sister nodded, her lips tightened. She heaved a sigh of relief. "So, I ask you, Biase: do you accept the adoption option or do you want to consult your home people before we take any further step?"

"Sister, my people are insensitive. When on one side I remember what I passed through, I hate them more and can never imagine keeping my babies in their care. When on the other hand I remember what that man did to me, I feel like killing him. He is dead though. I saw him faintly; I was very weak. I felt some pain and when he left, I heard him utter a sharp cry. In the morning I saw something like dried blood and pap between my thighs. That man destroyed me, he killed me he…"

Sister held Biase tight, feeling her whole body quake with deep sobs.

"Go easy, sweet angel, easy. It's happened already and you have emerged victorious. We should be thanking God for His mercies. I think God has been merciful to us. Don't you agree?" Biase nodded.

"Okay, wipe your tears." Biase obeyed and sat up again. There was silence as Sister looked at the girl with sympathy.

Biase heaved a deep sigh, hissed and continued, "No, they don't deserve my babies. Only over my dead body can that happen!"

"Please don't swear, Angel. Don't, I beg you. No matter what, don't swear. All our hope is in God Almighty."

With a strong frown on her face, Biase just stared at nothing.

"I accept the option of adoption, even though I feel pain. I also feel it is the best for me. I just want to move on. I agree with you, Sister, and believe that you will place the babies in the best of hands. Besides, I do not want to have constant reminders of that ordeal around me."

"Very well then, we'll proceed with the plans. I commend your intelligence and farsightedness. Rest assured that only capable hands will receive the babies."

"But Sister, do me a favour. Please delay it a bit so my mother can set her eyes on the babies. Please, Sister."

"Alright, angel, we'll do just that as long as it won't take long."

"No, Sister. It's in a couple of days."

As was usual with the Raboni's, they named the babies using their ballot naming system. Tiny tallies that had all the letters of the alphabet were joggled in a non-transparent nylon bag.

"Come on, Biase, dip your hand in the bag and pick a tally!" It was as if she was playing a game of Scrabbles with Mother Anthonia, who presided over the exercise. She dipped into the bag and picked a tile that had letter "I" on it. They all cheered.

"Now let's see. What are the 'I' names we can think of?" Mother Anthonia asked.

"Ignatius, Innocent..." the sisters proffered.

"Oh yes, Innocent would have been ideal if we had just one baby. As you all know these babies' mother is innocent. Let's try out other 'I' names. It looks like "I" names are difficult to come by."

"Ian, Istophanus, Ingrad."

"What about Isaac?" Biase asked.

"Wow! Isaac!" They jumped at the idea, making the victory fist.

"Yes, Isaac and Ishmael are biblical brothers, sons of Abraham!"

"Wow, how apt!" the nuns acclaimed, shaking hands with each other and hugging Biase, who just looked on.

Biase took a close look at her twins, carefully recording in her memory, every image and picture cut by the babies. She closed her eyes tight, letting out free streaming tears in strong sobs. The Sisters looked on with misty eyes, as Biase peered into the tiny faces of the babies. Tears flowed when Biase began to talk, clutching her belly.

"Only God knows why my womb was made to carry the sons of a rapist. Only God knows what these sons will turn out." She held on to their cribs. "My prayer is for God to bless this womb that carried the twins." She touched her belly. "And bless the twins also." Her hands went back to the cribs. "I know that I will miss you both, seriously. I love you deeply and want the best for you. That is why I am letting go." She looked up. "God Almighty, I place them in your care because I know that anything in your care is secure. I look up to you for total protection."

# CHAPTER SIXTEEN

## *Who? Who? Who?*

It was a blue sky on a Saturday morning. A big white Ford SUV drove into Naminsa, trailing behind a metallic saloon Toyota Camry, registration number CL 383 EKY, amidst cheers and waves from community members and shouts from children. The Toyota had members of FRAP and the Community News while the jeep had Rita, Mary, the babies, and Dr. Stapyioth. Mary of the Community News occupied the back seat with Rita, helping her with handling one of the babies. When the vehicles came to a stop at their destination, it was as if a trumpet sounded, calling on everybody to hands-off whatever they were doing and assemble at Oyiga's compound. They came to see for themselves. No one wanted to be told stories. They pushed and struggled to catch a glimpse of Rita and the twins. Nothing of the sort had ever happened in Naminsa. Community News recorded every move as the women burst into singing and dancing; releasing the joyous cry that usually heralded the birth of a new baby.

*If not for the child, I might have been blind*
*Who would have given to me?*
*Who would have clothed me?*
*My child is my legacy and hope*
*As long as there is life, there is hope.*
*The tree expected to fall is now upright, rooted firmly.*
*Thank you oil Oyibo for caring so lovingly*

*If not for the child, who would have given to me?*
*Who would have clothed me?*
*I might have been blind!*

Idiapa and his people had known that Rita's return was a matter of days, judging from the renovations carried out on the house and the speed with which it was done. But they did not know the exact day, so there was no preparation for a feast. Idiapa, after getting over the initial surprise, brought out a low table, covered it with white cloth and placed it at one corner of the compound. He brought chairs with which he surrounded the table, placing some drinks and tumblers on it. He invited Stapyioth and his team to sit for a drink. Now seated, Dr. Stapyioth watched the dancing women, smiling and nodding to the rhythm of their music. Also sitting around the table were a few of the community members including the two who had earlier paid a visit to Shores 2, with Idiapa.

"Welcome sir," Idiapa was facing Dr. Stapyioth, who grinned with contentment. "You can never imagine what favour you have done me and our community, Naminsa, neither can you imagine how thankful we all are. You see, my people always say that when mere thanks are not adequate, God takes over. I pray to God to take over with the appropriate reward for your generosity and goodwill."

"Thank you, Mr...?

"Silas. Idiapa Silas."

"Oh yes! Silas. Mr. Silas, the pleasure is ours. We also thank God. You see, we believe in God but we also believe in fairness to fellow humans. We would have been unfair to Mrs. Rita Silas if we had left her by the water shores where we found her on that day. We pray that God helps us all to learn to be fair to our fellow humans. Thanks for all what you have presented us with." Stapyioth gesticulated toward the low table covered with white cloth.

Clifford and Stapyioth each took a small shot of the liquor on the table while Paul and Johnny had some soft drinks and the community elders gulped a good quantity of the local gin. Mary had gone into Rita's renovated home with her. Soon after, another woman, Sophie's mother, came in and took the baby from her. Mary stepped outside and stood watching the women dancing. The music and dancing though spontaneous got more interesting as more people rushed to join in the rejoicing. Suddenly one woman rushed to the scene with a big jar of sweet scented white talcum powder and sprayed it on the women's necks and shoulders. Some of them preferred to collect the powder in their palms and apply to their faces. Idiapa had asked someone to go to the local kiosk to get some crates of soft drinks and packets of Cabin biscuits for the women dancers and on-lookers. Before the drinks arrived, some men had joined the women in the dance, spreading notes of money on their foreheads in admiration. On seeing this, Stapyioth got up and joined them to the amazement and delight of everybody. He was demonstrating his own unique dance steps, slightly different and out of rhythm from the women's music, but everybody appreciated his gesture and admired him, even more as he began spreading a higher denomination of money on the women's foreheads, an act that made the women scramble for his attention. Mary, Clifford and Paul tried out their dance footsteps and also performed the money spreading routine.

"Heey, Oyibo is dancing oh!" The people screamed when Stapyioth started dancing. Rita took some money from her hand bag, came out of the room and caught a glimpse of her beloved benefactor. Baby in one hand and dancing with joy, Rita spread a few notes on the forehead of a surprised Stapyioth, but that was tradition. Stapyioth gave Rita and baby a big hug amid smiles and laughter. As if to reciprocate Rita's gesture, Stapyioth placed several notes of money on both Rita and the baby. Sophie's mother who had joined in the dance received the same gesture, with the baby, from Stapyioth. Johnny was behind the camera, having fun his own way. No need to protect his camera from any assaults, this time. The women had stopped dancing now and were wiping away sweat with their wrappas. They sat on long wooden benches provided by Idiapa and took a bottle each, of the soft drink Idiapa offered them. They chattered and wondered how God works. One woman stretched her own wonder in the hearing of the others when she burst into a popular church song in Pidgin English and immediately the rest joined her.

*Dis God na wah oh*
*Dis God na wah oh*
*Dis God na wah oh*
*Dis God na wah oh*

*I neva see dis kind God before*
*Wonda wonda, wonda wonda*
*I never see this kind God before*
*Wonda wonda, wonda wonda*

Sophie was in the crowd of mainly young people who stood aside watching. She could not help feeling sorry for her friend Biase for missing out on all these. Immediately the party was over, she hurried to the Raboni's and told Biase everything that had happened and worked up her desire to see her mother as a matter of urgency but there was no way she could be allowed to leave the Home because she still nursed her child birth wounds. Sophie asked Biase not to worry as she was going right away to convey her feelings to her mother who she was sure would not wait to see her. She left hurriedly after the very brief meeting, and biked home straight to Biase's mother, panting.

"I told Biase that you are back," she announced, slightly out of breath.

"Oh my God, how is she? Is she still at that Home?"

"Yes. She is fine, she had twins too, they are…"

"Eeh! She had what? She did what? What do you mean? I mean, what did you just say? Sophie?"

"Biase was safely delivered of a set of male twins. They are doing very well. I got there on the day she had the babies."

"Doing well, male twins, safely delivered… Sophie, you are not making sense." Rita was pleading with Sophie, gesticulating with her hands.

"It's true ma. Biase gave birth to twins."

Dazed, Rita went silent, short of words. She threw herself on the solid cabinet bed provided by Shores 2. Two to three minutes slipped by and Rita had not said one word to Sophie, only just gazing at her as if receiving psychiatric therapy. She imagined everything and spoke after almost about five minutes.

"Was she pregnant?"

Sophie noticed that Rita was becoming almost uncoordinated and wondered how she could forget that any female delivered of a baby must have been pregnant.

"Yes, ma; she was raped."

Rita stood up and placed her hands on her head.

"Hei! Oh my God! Lord of mercy!" She was restless. Sophie thought she was now looking at a woman gone hysterical.

"Who? Who? Who raped her? Who raped my daughter? Why? Hey!"

As Rita paced about uttering those cries, one of her twins shifted tenderly, cuddling himself. Her eyes caught him and she lowered her voice, instantly. The baby went back to sleep and she began to think and wonder to herself. She resolved within herself that nothing short of rape could have caused such a pure damsel to be pregnant at her young age. She thought about the girl she brought up herself, who was pure up till the time they embarked on that journey; and further got convinced that she must have been raped. She got some reprieve from that conviction and spoke again to Sophie.

"She was raped?"

Sophie nodded cheerlessly and Rita stared at her, urging her with her hands, to speak on.

"Yes, ma. The same man that rescued her on the day of that accident took her to his family home and raped her while she was sleeping, very tired from the ordeal of the day. When uncle Idiapa discovered that she was pregnant, he asked her to leave his home. She tried to explain what happened but he would not listen, so I accompanied her to the Raboni's where they took care of her till she had her babies."

Rita broke down and wept. Sophie stepped out of the room and locked Rita in. And, running as fast as her legs could carry her, dashed into their home.

"Mummy, please come; there is a problem."

"What is the matter?"

"Come now. It's Biase's mother."

"Ah, what is wrong with Rita? Are her babies okay?" She rushed out of her house as she spoke, adjusting her wrappa. They soon got to Rita's house.

"See, Mama, I have the key, I locked the door."

"Why should you do that? Will you open that door quickly! Open, quickly!"

"Rita, what is the matter? What's going on?" Sophie's mother sounded jolted.

"Ha Eunice, can you listen to what your daughter is telling me? I am finished," Rita cried out, on sighting Eunice, her friend. Sophie's mother looked at her daughter and she repeated what she had told Rita.

"Oh, Rita, you are not thankful to God that your daughter is alive, eh? You are crying." She turned again to her daughter and said, "Okay, my dear, you may leave now. I'll soon join you." Sophie obliged and Eunice continued. "If she, and indeed you too, had drowned on that day, what mouth would you have used to cry? You know that Biase is quite demure and could never have misbehaved but she was attacked and," she took a breath, "cursed be whoever that attacker is, wherever he may be. You should also be happy that she went through pregnancy and child birth safely. And now, as if in a festival of twins, the supposedly barren woman has two sons and two grandsons. And you have the mouth to cry Rita. Please begin to wipe those tears and give God all the glory."

Rita beamed a light smile.

"Eunice, my friend, thank you very much. That is not the only anomaly breaking my heart about my daughter's plight. I don't even know which one hurts me more between the assault on Biase by the outsider, the boatman, and that of the insider, Idiapa and his wife."

"Now, you know. That's how people are. But come, Rita, have you forgotten so soon what happened before your travel to the riverine area?"

Biting her lower lip, Rita shook her head slowly. She tried to compare Idiapa's disposition of excitement on her arrival from the creeks with his indifference towards Biase when she needed their help. Closing her eyes, she visualised Idiapa's wife dancing with the other women in the crowd on the day she returned and wondered what bold-faced wickedness that was. Her mind went to her harvest of twins and she wondered how four boys would be brought up without fathers. Eunice looked on, letting her be.

"My dear, you need to lie down a little."

"Thanks Eunice." Rita heaved a heavy sigh. "You've been wonderful, Sophie too. I did not even know that she locked the door from outside to go and call you. I only heard you scolding her just before she unlocked it. Sweet girl, I'll ask her to take me to Biase tomorrow. In fact, I do not know how to thank that girl."

Eunice smiled, not saying anything. After spending a little more time with Rita, she left, making sure her friend was calm. With the twins asleep, Rita said to herself, *no wonder she looked bloated in the magazine picture.* And looking upward, she said "God, how much more hurt can I take? How will the babies be taken care of?" She felt the blood in her veins boiling. All of a sudden, she got up and marched to Idiapa's house. Idiapa opened his mouth and eyes but could not say anything.

"Idiapa, you think say all your wickedness merit God forgiveness?" she charged at him.

"Rita!" Idiapa's mouth remained open.

"No, no, no, make you no Rita me o. Wicked man!" She waved her right hand at surprised Idiapa, menacingly. Idiapa's wife had come from outside to find out what the noise was all about. Rita did not spare her either.

"And you! You dey call yourself mama wey dey go morning mass for 6 o'clock every day. Dem even give you big church award - Worthy Mother. Which kain worthy mother be dat?" Rita charged at her.

"Wetin I do you, Rita?" she asked, surprised.

"Wetin you do me? E no go beta for you. Wetin you do me? Wey my daughter, where you drive am go? Pikin wey for that time, e no get, mama e no get papa. E come for im papa brother place, na im you pursue am. Where you drive am go? And na girl o. Iniapre, you get conscience at all? Wey my pikin? God go punish you and your husband no be small. E no go beta for una, laiye laiye" Idiapa's wife could not find a place to hide her face.

"Biase carry bele come meet us; wetin we for do?" Iniapre, Idiapa's wife let out.

"If na your own pikin from your bele, wetin you for do? You ask Biase wetin happen? You ask am how e carry bele come? Na only God go judge you and your husband. Your husband drive my husband enter water wey kill am; Infact, your husband kill my husband, hin brother, you drive my pikin comot for your house. Even if na your husband say make Biase comot from im house, you wey be mama no for gree, if you be better mama, but na for God hand I leave una. Una must get una payment. Wicked people!" She was about to storm out when Idiapa grabbed her by the elbow.

"No vex, my wife. The trouble too much for us that time, no vex."

Rita burst into hot steaming tears, bending slightly as she wept, her hands cupped her face. Iniapre held her but she shrugged her off and stormed out of their house. She entered her apartment, locked the door and continued crying. When one of her babies began to cry, Rita knew that it was time for her to stop crying.

"You see what you have caused?" Idiapa said, turning to his wife.

"What did I do, Idi? Were you not the one that asked the girl to leave?"

"Were you not the one that told me she was pregnant? Do I know when a woman is newly pregnant? Couldn't you have asked her not to leave, couldn't you have convinced me? Look at her, Worthy mother indeed!"

"Look who's talking. Couldn't you be a real man and handle any situation that came your family's way, with maturity? Supposed and so called head of family. Ha!" She gesticulated mockingly towards her husband, with her lips and right palm thrusted towards him.

"Supposed, so called?"

"Yes, supposed, so called. After making a wrong decision, you do not want to take the responsibility that goes with it. You want to shift the blame to your wife. You should have asked me to take the decision. No be only head of family, na, tail of family. Nonsense!"

Idiapa glared at his wife, took a deep breath, sighed and moved into the inner room. Iniapre dragged a low bench noisily and sat on it, heaving a deep sigh.

"Come and blame me again for your mistake, let me see." She snapped her fingers towards him as he left.

The Sisters had not yet returned from morning mass when Sophie and Rita got to the Raboni's where another ceremony of tears began. For five minutes, mother and child were locked in an embrace without uttering a word. Only fast running liquid that could aptly be described as *more than tears*, rolled down their cheeks. When they finally unlocked the embrace and sat down looking straight into each other's eyes, Biase said as she sobbed, "Mummy, I did not do it. I was raped when…"

"Shh!" Rita placed her forefinger across Biase's lips. "I know. I trust you, my daughter. I believe you. I know you very well. Are you not my daughter? I know what you are capable of doing. Don't worry; I have heard everything that happened. Stop crying, okay? We must always move forward and never backward," she said wiping the tears off her daughter's eyes, with the tip of her wrappa.

"Where are the babies?" Rita asked.

"At the annex," Biase said. "Mummy, what are the names of my brothers?"

"Paul and Silas. I believe they prayed inside me and the Holy Ghost came down and prevented me from dying."

"Beautiful names and very meaningful too, even intriguing as one of them will be known as Silas Silas or Silas squared, or double Silas; doesn't that sound great mummy?"

"It does, my dear," Rita acknowledged, laughing for the first time since she stepped into the Home.

"Now that you are here, who is loking after them?"

"Who else could that be, Biase? I don't know how to thank Eunice and this, her daughter here with us." She was pointing at Sophie, who was all smiles.

"Sophie, please thank her for me?" Biase was indeed grateful.

"You are welcome.

When the sisters returned from morning mass, they took mother and daughter to see the babies – one to see her grandsons, the other her sons. Both spent some good time with the boys, noting the slight differences between them. They were not as identical as Rita's twins who both looked exactly like Oyiga. Rita tried in vain to hide her tears from Biase. Amid tears, she asked again to know who did that to her, daughter? Her hands up, Rita wailed uncontrollably. As her voice echoed, the whole ward vibrated.

"Oh God, why did you allow this to be my fate?" she pointed and looked upward. "My only daughter has just become a teenage mother, a mother of twins, courtesy of an ill-trained vagabond." And turning to her daughter, said, "Biase, I am taking these boys home. I will bring them up with Paul and Silas so they will be good boys. They will not be vagabonds! They will not be cursed like that animal who forced you. Four boys, like quadruplets. Yes, I will raise them. They will share everything with Paul and Silas, including my breast milk. I can do it. Bring them to me." She held Biase and drew her close to her, squeezing her tight, as if in a frenzy amid flowing tears. "My little girl, my baby, my one and only daughter, who did this to you? Who, who, who? It shall not be well with him but God who sees and knows all will grant you the grace to continue with your life. May God pave a way for you so you eventually reach your peak in all your endeavours, in spite of this setback." She left her daughter and went on her knees, raising her two hands up again. "Lord God, please grant this request, for in Jesus' name I have prayed!"

"Amen!" chorused Sophie and Biase.

Rita got up, her face all wet.

Biase managed to talk.

"Mummy it's okay. I am done with crying. You should be too. The future may be bright, who knows." Rita quickly wiped tears off her eyes and thanked Biase for being strong.

Mother and daughter discussed almost everything under the sun, within the period of the short visit, including the adoption idea. They both were not happy about it and wished they could do something about it – not with the impracticability of Rita, raising four babies, as a widow. Besides, the Reverend Sisters had taken her to a room where they also counselled her on how to take life at its pace and let God do the rest. Rita thought about Dr. Stapyioth and Shores clinic 2 and wondered if they would also want to take over the care of Biase's twins. She soon dropped the idea, not wanting to stretch her luck too far. She thought far and wide and came to terms with the idea of also letting go. The Sisters closely watched as she slowly turned to them.

"Okay! Sisters, I agree, especially as the 'mad' man responsible for the pregnancy is dead; and even if he were alive, he would not deserve to have those babies. My daughter may be too young to take that decision alone. I support her and add my voice to her decision. It is now our decision." Turning to her daughter, she said "Biase, my darling, you have your future to live out, nothing will stop you. Nothing, my baby, okay?" Biase nodded, feeling lighter.

They sorrowed together, licked their wounds and continued with life. Rita's breasts felt heavy and overflowing with milk, signaling time to feed the babies who, she was sure, were more than ready. They stepped out.

# CHAPTER SEVENTEEN

## The Five Bs

Two tributaries from one river had been formed. Isaac and Ishmael were fostered to two different homes. The Sisters gave out babies for adoption only when it was evident they would have a better life than otherwise. That meant prospects of good education, shelter, healthcare, nutrition, clothing, love and more. There had to be proof of adequate income and fine character, and good references before a baby is entrusted to the care of any family. Isaac and Ishmael were only fostered when these precautions had been taken, and Biase was set to move on with her life. She had not completed her Raboni-organised spiritual and academic lessons, where residents' capacity was built on religious and academic matters. The clinic had certified her okay to move back to the Home and come back for check-ups. On the appointed day, Biase sat waiting for the clinic's visiting doctor.

"Mothers who could not suckle a baby for one reason or the other have this problem, but not to worry, you'll get over it soon, the prescriptions work," the doctor assured her. "I'll see you again in two weeks' time."

Two weeks later, the doctor was amazed how fit Biase felt. She was fast getting back into her normal shape and one could hardly know that she had gone through the labour room. Her sore breasts had healed. Sophie, who had gone to check on her friend, had noticed that Biase already felt some relief.

"It's class-free tomorrow, Sophie. I long to spend the day with Mum and my brothers, you know, my other twins." Sophie looked beyond the forlorn appearance on Biase's visage, and saw pain so thick that it could be cut with a knife.

"We'll go together, Biase. I'll come and accompany you."

Biase could not utter a word. She simple got up slowly and gave Sophie a tight hug. Sophie understood the words spoken through that hug, letting out a short smile of empathy. They hurried into the Silas compound, making conscious efforts to avoid people. Biase could not help looking around. Her lower lip dropped in awe at the approach of their new home. Stepping into the house, she stood stunned.

"Sit down, my daughter. There is a little blessing in every disappointment. That's life. As long as there is life, there is hope. I wish Oyiga had life and hope instead of that unfortunate finality called death. But not to worry, all will be well." As she wiped a tear, Biase hugged her and emptied hers on her, while Sophie stood there like the secondary smoker, who inhales and is made uncomfortable by the smoke from the actual smoker.

She looked on, eyes wet, her presence assuring. Biase picked up one of the babies, looked into his tiny face and her heart melted with joy. Each time she held any of the babies in her hand, she became unwilling to lay him back in the crib even when the baby had fallen asleep in her arms. She had noticed the cute cribs provided by Shores 2.

"They are beautiful, mum, the cribs."

"Oh yes, my daughter, those 'good Samaritans' provided everything for the babies. God will surely reward them."

"They are unbeatable. Biase, you needed to have been here on the day they came. Everywhere was agog. They came with so much love and warmth. We were all dancing," Sophie said.

"Really? Hmm! I missed that one, but with these babies, I don't miss anything. I have not lost anything. True, Sophie, there is nothing to miss."

"I know."

Biase's eyes scouted almost every object in the house, as if on inspection. She was instantly beginning to feel part of her home again but loathed so much the presence of Idiapa and his wife within the compound. She could hear their voices from Rita's place; the sound of their movements too.

"I am hearing the voices of daddy's brother and his wife. Mum, I will never visit or greet them. I hate them." Hatred was written all over her.

"I don't blame you, Biase. I'd do the same if I were you. They are very wicked." Sophie's esprit de corps was unparralled.

But Rita intervened.

"Elders must be respected no matter what one has against them."

Biase had to soften her stance.

Rita herself exchanged greetings with them as if they were business partners and was not keen on their recent interest in associating with her. She always tried not to hold any grudge against anybody but forgetting what they did to her family was difficult. Life had to go on as if all were normal.

"Biase, I'll come back in the afternoon. Let me see what Mum is doing," Sophie said as she prepared to saunter home.

That shuttle from the Raboni Home to her home became Biase's most cherished assignment, the best thing that happened to her in recent time. It was amazing how her case was not blown open. The community people had heard that she survived the boat mishap. The few people who heard about her pregnancy were not cork sure. They never saw her pregnant at any time, so the story was that Biase was away somewhere and had now come back. She only looked slightly robust to them but as time went on, Biase and Rita returned to their old selves. Biase could now fit freely into her few old clothes but she, from time to time had an inexplicable and awkward feeling that she was a teenage mother of twins, who had given up her babies.

"Will I ever, ever see them again?" she wondered. Emotions welled up in her and she broke out in fresh tears. Whenever this happened to her, she remained moody all day and this worried her mother.

"No, Biase dear, not again, you must let go now; it's okay." She had once told her: "Begin to think of what next you want to do with your life. I abhor the idea of giving up babies but no one is prepared to handle the challenges in this case. We are totally unprepared for this and if the difficulties are not properly managed, anything can happen. My desire is for the babies to be alive in good hands and I trust Raboni to ensure that. Life is more important than any bravado urge to attempt something we are incapable of handling. I allowed it because there is no need to pretend my dear. There is also no need for an imagined but erroneous 'I can do it' stance which some might wish to adopt. Relax my daughter; let's see where providence takes us."

They looked into each other's misty eyes and understood that they must be consoled by the inability created by fate. Rita wiped her daughter's face, gave her a pat on the back and got her some water to drink."

"Mummy, will I ever be able to further my education, get married, have other children and settle properly in life?"

"Yes, of course, you will." Biase looked at her mother and she encouraged her further, "I'm positive. Nothing can be surer, Biase. You are beautiful, brilliant, brawny, brainy and 'Biasy'. I am tempted to call you a 'B' material but I think you're more like an 'A' material."

"Mummy!' Biase cheered, with a tint of excitement.

"Trust me, baby girl." Rita had her own way of injecting courage in her daughter's system.

Biase dashed to twin Silas who had started crying, picking him up from the crib and singing to him.

"Stop baby stop oh"

"Do not cry oh"

"You will be a fine boy"

"Stop, stop, boy"

She kissed her brother's cheek, singing and dancing with him, swaying him to the left and to the right. She looked at him and thought she saw him smile. Her pain melted away gradually. Time passed. Twins Paul and Silas were now about six months old. Biase had remained steadfast in her tutorials at the Raboni's, which were designed to lead to the award of a diploma certificate. She looked forward to receiving it. Sister Konsolina's eyes had followed Biase everyday, scrutinsing her every move and trying to squeeze out time to sit with her for a chat.

"Come with me, my angel. How have you been feeling?" Sister Konsolina stretched her right hand across Biase's back, holding and squeezing her shoulder as they walked to her office.

"Very well, Sister, thank you."

"God bless you, angel. Please sit down."

"Thank you, Sister."

"You are welcome, angel. I have news for you." Sister spelt out, staring at Biase, whose eyes dilated in apprehension.

"Good. Our foreign affiliate body, an international relief non-governmental organisation has a yearly scholarship policy which enables bright residents to attain higher education. You qualify for this award and we have sent your name to the institution. What do you have to say?" Biase stood up and unconsciously began to jump up and down, hands fisted, to Sister Konsolina's surprise and delight.

"It's a scholarship to study Sociology and Anthropology in a university abroad. I can see you welcome the idea. Would you like to study Sociology? It is a great course but most people unfortunately do not quite know this fact. It is a background course for every other course. In fact, everybody should be made to know a little bit of it at least."

"Thank you, Sister. I like it, a lot."

"You will be made to take a short academic test after which if you are successful, you'll be awarded the scholarship."

"When will the test be? I think I am ready. Sister, I will pass the test."

"That's my angel. May the good Lord continue to be your strength!"

Biase received and claimed that prayer and less than one year into the course at the Raboni's, Biase was awarded the scholarship to study Sociology and Anthropology in the US. Her mother could not explain why she panicked when the news hit her. Biase felt her apprehension and it was her turn to counsel her mother.

"Mum, it is hard for me too but I'll go. Please let me get away from this environment. Let me go and study and prepare myself to take care of you and my brothers, let me go and get back my life. I am excited but when I remember you and Paul and Silas, my zeal is dampened."

"Hm hm, don't allow it. We'll be fine. I'll be praying for you and you'll see, God will go there with you and you will find His favour."

"Amen, Mum!"

"Does Sophie know about it?" Rita tried to be cautious.

Biase nodded.

"Don't worry, Mum. Sophie is very discrete."

"Good. We'll tell your uncle on the very day you'll leave,"

"Do we need to even tell him?"

"Yes, baby girl, for posterity's sake. Meanwhile, continue with all the arrangements with the Raboni group."

Eventually when all her travel documents were ready, through the active assistance of the Raboni Sisters, Biase was ready to leave the shores of her fatherland. Fr, Lazarus came in to hold a mass for the residents and Biase's name was mentioned for prayers. The mood at the airport was something else. Sisters Konsolina and Callista were there, beaming with smiles, happy for Biase, who did not appear as happy.

"Hmm, I cannot leave you oh. Who will I stay with over there? Who will take care of me like you? Who am I going to meet there? I am so scared. I just hope I will not fall into evil hands again. I can't leave you."

The nuns were wiping their tears now. Konsolina was more discrete about it while Callista cried out in sobs. Konsolina held Biase in a tight hug and used a white handkerchief to mop the wetness on her face.

"Biase, the Lord goes with you, don't forget. We told Him everything in prayers. You will not be alone. Be confident, be faithful, look up to God and be serious with your studies, and before long, you'll be done."

A repeat announcement of the flight's departure came and Callista rushed to Biase and held her tight without uttering a word. It was Konsolina that spoke.

"You must leave now. Bye, angel. Have a safe flight."

"Thank you, Sister Konso, bye. Bye, Sister Callista." She waved as she spoke and they waved back at her. They watched her approach the entrance to the lounge and saw her turn to look at them and wave again. They reciprocated and within minutes Biase was seated in the aircraft. It was her first time in an aircraft and she found herself thanking God for the upliftment and the Reverend Sisters, Mother, Father and the Home for their nurture and benevolence.

She soon found great solace in her course work at the renowned Dade University, Miami Florida, in the United States of America. Biase realised that she was, after all, not a totally unlucky girl. She loved the several excursion tours organised by Dade and enjoyed all the fun sites in Florida. The beaches took her mind back to her days of sadness. The International Relief Organisation's scholarship usually provided enough cash for the solvency of its awardees. She could therefore visit home once a year as the extra cash added benign winds to her sails. She sensed that the annual visit home was a boost to her healing. One of her holidays coincided with the death of Iniapre, Idiapa's wife. The woman suddenly developed a malignant tumor below one of her ears and before they knew it, she died, leaving behind her not-too-young children and husband. During her funeral, Rita helped to prepare meals for Idiapa's family during the first few weeks. Biase was there to handle the babies. She also made some cash donations to Idiapa, which took care of some items for the funeral.

Sympathisers thronged Idiapa's house.

"My brother, take heart. It's one of those things."

"Thanks, brother" Idiapa replied.

One of them, Jenga moved closer to him and added rather insensitively, "You must be a man and take whatever fate brings your way but please try not to keep alone for too long. A man must not become a eunuch in the process of mourning his wife."

Idiapa was unprepared for that comment which was however commonplace and accepted in Naminsa. Nobody questioned it; it was as normal as male promiscuity. Even if anyone tried to, the usual "same soup" theory was usually expounded – no man eats the same soup everyday and remains sane. Rita, Eunice, Remane and others had nevertheless decided that not 'changing soup' was a healthy choice, and wished it could be adopted by all.

Rita had a piece of noteworthy information for her daughter. She had already told her that the CNN crew still visited her.

"Really, mother? Those people are wonderful. I like that Mary. I must get them all some gifts when next I visit."

"They keep me updated with what's going on around. They even have news about that riverine Piopio community."

"You mean Pionto Mum? Do I want to hear about that community? Mum, I don't think I want to hear about them?"

"My daughter, this is quite curious. You know that your life has been a lesson to a great many, especially the people of Naminsa." Biase shrugged. " The same also goes for the people of Pionto, Kruso's people." Biase looked at her mother. "When the CNN told them that Kruso's assault on you resulted in pregnancy which you carried till full term, his mother was eager to know more. When told that the pregnancy resulted in twins, she went frantic and sought to know where they were. She committed suicide after she was told that the two boys were given up for adoption and could never be hers."

"Oh no, I feel for her. I still remember the hot fresh fish pepper soup she fed me with on that day, even though I could not eat much. But in all honesty, my heart does not grant them ownership of those babies at all. Instead my heart goes to that Stapyioth hospital and wonders if we can pay them a visit. I can swim like fish now. I took swimming lessons in school, both theory and practicals. Also I just wonder why life jackets did not appear to be popular when we had that accident. It is all over the US for use by people who cannot swim."

"I see. That's unfortunate. I still cannot swim, but it's not as if boats capsize every day. We'd arrange a visit to them when next you visit. I just thought you should hear that bit about Piopio."

"It's Pionto, Mummy. It's a pity. May her soul rest in peace!"

"Amen!

## CHATER EIGHTEEN

### *Volumes*

"I finally said yes to Sompro. We'll be getting married in December." The e-mail message was clear.

"Wow! This is good news, Sophie. We'll all be home for you in December, God willing. Congratulations!" Biase sent back a quick reply.

Biase never lost touch with her confidant. Many times when she felt like talking with her mother, Sophie and the rest, she was grossly handicapped because those she wished to speak with had no phones asmat that time. Sophie checked her mail at the Raboni's once or twice weekly and in the process, developed interest and undertook a computer literacy course at its Computer Center. They had exchanged home and foreign news for about a year and Biase had thought it wise to send to her friend, university admission forms to be completed and sent back. Biase was prepared to send her friend initial funds that would assist her move over to Biase's school for studies but Sophie was not able to catch up with that pace. Biase knew all along that her friend was not as career-oriented as she was but still tried to give her some push. Sophie seemed to have a bigger capacity for homemaking and Biase was genuinely happy for her. She made sure she bought mobile phones for all of them so they could talk although she was the one who always called them.

It was Sophie's traditional wedding day. The people of Obosima, Sophie's suitors, had come and stood on the other side of the traditional wedding tape, ceremonially tied to two posts across the entrance gate to their compound.

"Our in-laws have arrived, let us go and welcome them," one of the elders beckoned at the others. They walked gracefully to their own side of the tape.

"You are welcome, our in-laws. We have been expecting you. We shall not keep you waiting. Your wife will come to usher you in, shortly. We welcome you, great in-laws."

"We thank you. Please tell our wife that we have come as promised."

"Exactly!"

Some maidens began singing and dancing toward the tape, behind which stood the visiting in-laws. One of them had her face covered from the head and Sophie's suitor looked at her, blinking several times. On getting to the tape, the maidens greeted the visitors and the lady with the covered face unveiled herself slightly and said, looking at them, "I welcome you my, husband; and your people..."

"No, this is not my wife. This is not the woman I came for. Please bring me my wife," Sompro interrupted, casting quick glances at his entourage.

"This is not the person we came for."

"I am your wife. I have prepared myself just for you. You cannot say I am not your wife. Am I no longer your heartthrob? Take a good look at me." She spun herself round and faced the crowd again. Sompro shook his head slowly and surely.

"You are not my wife, please go away. My wife is Sophie. You people should get me Sophie."

"I am Sophie!"

"You are not Sophie!"

"Is your so called Sophie prettier than I am?

"Get me my Sophie!"

"Fine, then. You must pay my transport fare to this place and for my return home, since you have rejected me." Sompro dipped his hand into his pocket and gave her a thousand naira note. She grabbed it.

"Thanks but this is not enough. It cannot take me home. You have inconvi..."

"You take another thousand and let me be. Please go now, okay."

He handed her another bill. She bluffed up to those in his entourage and they too dipped their hands in their pockets just to get the 'stumbling block' out of the way. She left, grudgingly but with a handful of naira notes, and the visitors heaved a happy sigh of relief.

"Hmm! Heey! Everybody hear this oo! He has rejected her! He has just said that Nma is not Sophie, and so, not his wife," one of the maidens announced screaming atop her voice. The same group of maidens led another lady to the visiting group, still singing and dancing.

As the lady raised her cover, Sompro exclaimed, "That's my wife! That's Sophie!" Shouts of joy rented the air. By Sophie's right hand side, another lady had a ribboned tray on which rested a pair of scissors. Sophie picked up the scissors, cut the tape and hugged her suitor.

"Welcome, Sompie. Welcome all!" Sophie flashed a smile and waved her hand, as the people cheered.

The music that had been low-toned now reverberated. The drummers themselves appeared excited. The maidens led the visitors to the canopy specially mounted for them. Everybody danced and appreciated each other, exchanging cash gifts as they danced. After a while, when they had fulfilled all other traditional requirements and it was time to go with their bride, Sophie tried not to cry but her mother's tears streamed. And hers flowed too. Her sibling managed not to shed tears in public. They looked beaten. Her father had died when she was 12 years old. One of her uncles had acted in his stead. Sophie was quite understood when Biase sent a message that she could not be at the traditional wedding due to exigencies of duty.

At 27, Biase had already spent over eight years abroad and had completed her doctoral studies after studying hard. Convocation day had African and Nigerian visitors swarming the venue, having come to cheer graduating relatives and friends.

"Hey, wouldn't it be great if all of us Nigerians here came together for a group photograph to cheer our graduating compatriots?" someone in the crowd suggested to the delight of all.

"Yes o, up Nigeria! Up Naija! All Nigerians, group photograph please!"

As Biase and her friends posed with others for the photographer, he directed the positioning of the excited Nigerians.

"One man, one woman!" he instructed, insisting on a one-female one-male line up, before snapping. He clicked on his camera over and over again.

"One more time," he said, and added, "more smiles please."

Nigerians who did not know one another all enjoyed each others' laughter and smile. The man standing next to Biase helped to adjust the collar of her dress.

"Sorry, may I?" he asked.

"Oh thanks," Biase appreciated, noticing him for the first time.

"You are so beautiful," the man said, looking at her with intent, his eyes and lips curving into a disarming smile. Biase was at a loss. Did she blush? Biase had a beautiful dark and unblemished skin that glistened in harmony with her pure beauty. She managed to utter a 'thanks so much,' avoiding his eyes. But the man stretched out his right hand to her and introduced himself.

"I am Lande Dagama."

"Biase Silas." Biase responded as they shook hands.

"Silas, which part of the country is the name from?" Lande pried.

"Naminsa; a non-riverine community in South East Nigeria."

"That's about 10 kilometers from my hometown. I am from Kwasama, one of Naminsa's neighbouring communities."

"It's a lie," Biase did not know when that escaped from her lips. She quickly added, slightly nervous and surprised that anybody that close could so easily be met in a part of the world so distant from hers:

"I am sorry. I didn't mean to, it's just that em, it's em, it's surprisingly close."

"No. I call it providence. Tamiya over there is my maternal cousin and I came around to witness her day of glory." His index finger pointed towards Tamiya.

"Oh! She is my course mate and friend."

"All in place, right? The jigsaw will soon be solved." Lande looked around and waved at Tamiya who was engrossed in chats with others. Tamiya caught his glance and waved back. Lande signaled her to come over.

"Tami, I've been having some good time with someone very interesting. Says she's your friend. I like her."

"Hmm, that's good. Biase, I hope you like my cousin as well. Am I hearing wedding bells soon?" she asked, winking at Biase with hearty laughter.

"Tami will you shut your...," Biase jeered.

"Okay o, I will for now, but..." Tamiya pulled away from them, heading for her chat group but turned and said, "But I will talk on your wedding day o, remember that. You might not be able to stop me then. Ha! Ha! Ha! See you later." Tamiya dashed off. Biase sighed and waved her away.

"Crazy cousin of mine," Lande said.

Biase smiled and hissed again, trying not to look at Lande. She felt like escaping yet she felt like spending more time with Lande. He seemed to have seen through her thoughts.

"Come on," he said, holding her hand. "Let's talk more over a snack and drink." They walked along and Biase drew his attention to a stand.

"Oh yes, we can sit here. I'll get you a burger and a soda." Biase nodded and within minutes, they were both having a bite. He drove her home and promised to be back. Biase did not seem able to get the young man off her mind. She had never felt that way before and could not fathom what was going on with her. It looked like the same bug had bitten Lande as he paid Biase daily visits after work. And each time, they sat outside the college apartment rented by Biase.

"You must visit my house today," Lande said to her, rather softly.

"Must?"

"No, not at all, I'll love you to just come and know my place."

"Do I have to?"

"Oh baby!" his eyes spoke volumes.

"I think we can stay here and chat and... whatever." Biase shrugged.

"Okay, if you say so, but..."

"Excuse me. Just a minute, I'll be back." Biase walked away, heading for the apartment. Sitting alone outside, Lande's eyes studied the environment. Biase emerged dressed in a blue Jeans skirt and pink top, with her hair tucked back in a knot. She wore little or no makeup and had a pair of stud earrings that was close neither to gold nor silver. Lande had a surprise look on his face.

"Let's go," she announced.

"Go where?" Lande was confused.

"To your house."

"To my..." Lande stood up, pointing at himself. He laughed and gave Biase a big hug.

"That was quite naughty," Lande touched her nose and she eyed him.

Biase thought she liked Lande's small apartment but had within minutes discovered its several flaws as her eyes took quick glances around. Lande had gone into his kitchen and had come out with a rectangular tray of some exquisite biscuits and drinks which they both took, chatting heartily. Afterwards they took a drive round the small but exciting town of Port Louis before Lande took Biase back to her apartment. Later, their meetings became frequent and on one occasion when Biase cleaned up and fixed Lande's apartment, the young man was speechless. It was as if his tongue got a new lease of life when Biase fixed lunch.

Biase kept no secret from Lande, a 32-year-old who had also finished his studies and was already working. She told him everything about her past in a fashion that smacked of 'this is me, nothing hidden; take me as I am or leave me.' This bold move made Lande Dagama more interested in—and proud of—Biase, whom he married one year after their first meeting. They returned to Nigeria to formalise their union according to tradition. Her uncle, Idiapa, stood in for her late father and enjoyed all benefits that accrued from the customary formalisation. *Custom is an ass*, Biase thought. But remembering her success in spite of all that happened in the past, she recoiled and brought back her happy mood.

Biase and Lande had agreed they would skip the bride-kneeling-in-the-crowd ritual. They agreed that as a forward-looking couple, they would go for less threatening ways of presenting the marriage drink. This came up when Biase reminded Lande that they were both not brought up in a culture of kneeling except in punishment or prayers, unlike in some cultures where from childhood boys and girls were made to imbibe the culture of prostrating and kneeling. For those boys and girls, that culture had become part of them.

"It reminds me of those days when daddy punished me for not scoring a high mark in a subject, or mummy reminded me to say, 'Our Lord's Prayer.' Both chores required me to kneel and I never hesitated. It bothers me that at 28, I am going to perform that act again, this time, neither in punishment nor in prayer. Sweetheart, how do you perceive that?"

Spotting a genuine smile and taking hold of his fiancée's hand, he stared at her with intensity as she spoke, looking beyond her physical self, sensing her sheer nature, the purity that was Biase, and shaking his head from side to side while holding her hand.

"No way, no such thing, darling; it's too lopsided," Lande said in a low tone, giving Biase a soft peck on the cheek.

On that day, Biase paced on gracefully, looking into the crowd, searching for Lande, to present him with the marriage drink. It was her traditional wedding day and her right hand was clutching a gourded cup, with her left palm covering the mouth of the cup.

"It's me. I'm the right man. Give me the drink," some young men in the audience jested, stretching out their hands. She ignored them and continued her search for Lande, who had sneaked away from his seat, behind the seated guests, who wondered what he was up to. He made for the arena and tip-toed up to just behind his damsel. The awed spectators gazed, not knowing what to make of the new unfolding picture. Biase had graceful dance steps, which she combined with the search. She looked left and right, seeking to locate her suitor, still holding on to the cup with wine in it, for him. She continued to ignore the 'impostors.' Lande was now close to her, right behind her. Stepping up, Lande from behind gently placed his palms across her eyes, blind-folding her momentarily, amid cheers and laughter from the crowd. When he lifted his palms, she turned around and saw him. They hugged and the people cheered.

"Hmm, children of nowadays, they never cease to amaze me. See how they have introduced a new dimension to this ceremony. Quite interesting, I must say, I'm indeed thrilled," one of the elders said.

"Aha, our young ones sure know how to entertain us," another concurred and added, "these ones are from abroad, no wonder they came with a fresh delight, truly entertaining."

Away from the elders, some young men also made their comments: "This is good, o boy, I'll do mine exactly the same way, when the time comes.

"Yes, me too. Ah! This is a fine deviation from the old and monotonous way of doing it. Looking back now, it appears clumsy to me – searching for me while I sit there like Humpty Dumpty, finding me and going down on both knees to present the drink to me. The same practice, over and over again. Kai!"

Lande took the drink from Biase, took a gulp and placed the cup between her lips, holding her closely. More cheering as she drank. Then he held Biase by the hand and led her to the elders, handing back the cup to them, after he had dropped some cash in it. Now, they both knelt and the elders, including Idiapa, blessed the couple, who got up and proceeded to the dance floor, moving to traditional music from drums and gongs. Rita, her mother hopped into the dance arena, possessed by joy, and danced as if that was all she knew how to do. Several people joined them, dropping some cash gifts as they danced.

Lande walked Biase to the canopy reserved for the couple and their friends, and as they strolled to the canopy, Biase whispered to him, "You are truly a man of your words. Thanks, my love!" Biase's eyes sparkled as she spoke.

"How can I belong to the group of fellow young men who, in spite of all their education still have their mentality soaked in some culture that is blind to people's feelings. Well, we have to educate them and that is what I think we just did."

"Congratulations! You did it in style." Someone hailed.

"Thank you."

"I really liked the deviation," Lande's friend, Jerry, said." It's amazing how we allow ourselves to get soaked in dulling cultures and believe that it is the right thing to do. Lande mhen, you opened my eyes today, you and your wife. Thank you."

"The pleasure is ours, Jerry."

Everybody was now eating and enjoying the ceremony but Jerry, not quite settled, dropped the cutlery and talked again, "I wonder why people take delight in watching a bride in her traditional wedding attire go down to present a drink or in her Western style wedding gown, at the wedding reception, just to put a piece of cake in the groom's mouth. Gosh! A piece of cake! And the groom feels good about it?"

Lande and Biase exchanged familiar looks as Jerry talked. Jerry spoke on.

"No one has all that time now. Just watch, it will die a natural death. People should start talking about these practices otherwise, the ladies will continue to pretend to enjoy it, so as to be labelled good and the men will continue to receive the eye service honour that follows it. Think about it, who is actually fooling who? This does not take anyone anywhere." Lande and Biase looked on, speechless wondering if their traditional wedding was not turning into a seminar. Jerry, the supposed seminar speaker, asked:

"Are the most important ingredients in marriage not mutual love, mutual trust and mutual respect, and not any pretentious public show? Just the three mutuals!" he flashed three fingers before them.

"Have you tried to see the symbolism of that practice?" Lande's other friend, Densum asked, while his girlfriend looked on, listening.

"What symbolism, other than to remind one party of being the inferior one? We should all be reminded that no human being is inferior. But it is good to note that nobody should be forced, it should all be optional." Jerry fired back.

The Raboni Sisters had sat quietly in the area reserved for them. They had watched all proceedings with delight. Biase was their *pet project* so they had to be there to witness her day. Biase and Lande got up and went to their corner to pay their courtesies. The Sisters all stood up to honour the couple, to the delight of all. It was no longer a secret that they had cared for her in her time of need. They gave her an envelope.

"Take this little something for kolanuts and garden eggs.

"Congratulations, Biase! We are indeed happy for, and proud of you. We have been well entertained and would be leaving now. Send our kind regards to your mum and brothers. We had earlier exchanged greetings with them." They all hugged her one after the other and Lande watched on, overrun by emotions. The couple watched them move gracefully towards the exit, most of them very shapely, in their nun's attire. At the gate, they all turned to wave at Biase and Lande, who waved back enthusiastically. The two gently walked back to their seat.

"How nice of them to have honoured the occasion," said Lande.

"Oh they are always faithful to their cause," Biase confirmed.

"We must visit them again. When do you think we can do that?" Lande added with eagerness. She had earlier gone to the Home with Lande to introduce him to them and invite them to the traditional marriage.

"As early as we can. You know I have not given them the gifts I got for them"

"Can we go tomorrow then?

"Day after."

"Okay," Lande concurred.

# CHAPTER NINETEEN

## *Solace*

Lande and Biase returned to the US after the traditional ceremony and began a new life together. They had held a small but rich church wedding in Port Louis, after their visit to the Registry. One year of their union produced a lovely daughter who Biase aptly named Solace because according to her, that daughter was the one who came with the final drop of oil that completely calmed the turbulent ocean of her life. She looked at the baby and heaved a sigh of relief.

"Thank you for completing what Lande had started." She must have thought the baby was listening to her.

While in school, she had no idea what area of specialty she would adopt after her first degree in the broad field of Sociology and Anthropology. The wings of destiny however took her to undergo a specialist course in Conflict Resolution, which she assiduously followed for twelve months. Little did she know that on completion of the specialist training, a bigger job awaited her at a subsidiary office of the United Nations, where the developing world fell within her portfolio. Her new office controlled several sections, all dealing with various developing world issues. Biase was, in accordance with her area of specialisation, posted to a section that dealt with conflict resolution. Brokering peace and providing succour became her specialty at the International Relief Organisation and Biase was one of the Oversight Advisors for the African continent. The office handled crises and conflict resolution for the developing world section of the United Nations. The job entailed travelling regularly to Africa, including her own country, Nigeria; as well as initiating peace moves where necessary, on behalf of the United Nations. In every conflict-prone country she went, she started an action that set the peace process in motion. She soon became the pride of the office and, "that's no problem, our Oversight Advisor will handle it" became a catch phrase in the organisation.

As she tirelessly worked on a series of reports, her laptop always close by, it looked like she had become addicted to the machine. Sometimes when she worked at home, her husband complained and advised her to give the computer a break. Whenever that happened, Biase knew that the man was simply longing for her attention. She winked at him, saved her work and put the computer aside to attend to his needs. Her husband, an infotech personnel, understood the addictive power of the computer and did not bear his wife any grudge. Biase herself was quick to make amends whenever she saw certain signs. Lande had gone further in his Systems Engineering specialty, becoming a manager in a renowned Information Technology firm.

When another baby girl came their way, they named her Goladinu, translated to mean 'Golden', because they had envisioned their union as golden. When later their third child arrived, he was called Vutchita, meaning Victor; they figured that looking back at their lives so far, they could indeed claim victory.

Solace, Golden and Victor were their most cherished treasures. SGV, the collective name they coined for the three of them, could be heard in the house uncountable times daily.

"Lande, I am off to the super mart, see you later," Biase had informed her husband.

"Shopping again? You were there just two days ago."

"Yeah, this time, it's specifically for SGV needs. Keep an eye on them; I'll be back soon."

"Okay, see you then."

# CHAPTER TWENTY

# Bad News Everywhere

In the Dagamas' home country, in Nigeria, there was a deepening of ethno-religious strife, and as they both read about it in the newspapers and watched news about it on the television, they were saddened by the senseless destruction of lives and property that always followed the disturbances.

"There is an absolute lack of wisdom in compatriots, slaughtering each other like animals. I sincerely pray and hope for a quick end to these horrors." Biase was quite vocal on this issue.

"I can't stand the press hype here. The way they harp on the happenings puts me off. Besides, I think they tend to blow them out of proportion. Did you notice the look on the newscaster's face yesterday a she mentioned the number of people killed in a church in Nigeria?"

Biase nodded.

"Each time I listen to or watch news from Nigeria, I get very uncomfortable and the next day when my office colleagues take me up on it, I am usually at a loss and gripped by shame."

After church service on Sundays, they stood around with friends and their other compatriots in the Diaspora to share similar concerns.

"Whenever they start reporting those horrors, I feel pain, most times because of the derogatory manner in which they go about it. I must tell you this, it deflates whatever pride I have in me," Bernard

Uguru lamented. His wife's face had an obvious frown just like every other face there.

"It is indeed an issue of major concern. My colleague's brother was among those who died in the most recent attack. She just could not hold herself when she heard the news. A scene was created by her reaction when she passed out momentarily. Apparently not knowing that Bridget had not heard the bad news, someone called to commiserate with her."

"Oh so sorry about that. Must have been very hard for her," one of them commented.

"Hmm. I am trying hard to decipher what their grouse is. What drives them and why they take delight in killing other humans," Biase said and the others shrugged, knowing that nothing may come out of that thought, especially as the attacks took various forms, ranging from arson, bomb blasts and suicide bombings to rapes, shooting and beheading.

Back home some conscientious Nigerians, the True Patriots, also felt genuine concern about the issue and sought to do something about it. These concerns were quite often published in the newspapers but unfortunately, they had always remained concerns, on the pages of newspapers. The insurgence reoccurred often proving too tough for the government of the day.

There had been tremendous pressure from internal and external fronts, on the leader of the nation, the President, to do something decisive on ethno-religious intolerance in the country. He summoned his council members and charged them to brainstorm and bring him suggestions on how to tackle the monster. No one told the council members that when the source of a stream gets agitated, the whole stream becomes equally agitated.

The next meeting with the President was in four days' time.

"Your Excellency, there is a certain Nigerian, Biase Dagama, resident in the U.S. who has specialised in counselling and brokering peace between conflicting groups. Her exploits and antecedents have become widely known, as I found out in my broad search. She specifically oversees African countries," Namuke announced.

"How authentic?" the President wanted to know.

"Internet sources, sir. I browsed for quite a while, visiting different sites. She has huge credentials."

"A Nigerian?"

"Yes, Your Excellency"

"Female?"

"Yes sir."

"Quite interesting!"

"Your Excellency, with due respect to Honourable Namuke's efforts, I think a man would make a better option for this job. I suggest we keep the woman on standby and search further for a man," one of the members suggested.

"How can we reach her?" The President asked Namuke.

"I downloaded necessary information that can help us reach her, sir. She was born here but left our shores some years ago."

Everyone seemed to have taken advantage of the ensuing silence to ruminate over Namuke's proposal. The member who wanted a further search now looked dejected. The President, breaking the silence, sought the views of other council members. The consensus was that it should be given a trial.

"Thanks, Namuke, for this information." He turned to Namuke, "Please forward every useful information to Protocols, while the search continues. We must not put all our eggs in one basket. Have I made myself clear?"

"Very clear, Your Excellency," they chorused.

When other items on the agenda were exhausted, the Council rose.

The President's directives on contacting Biase were immediate and to the point:

> "Go and look for her wherever she is and tell her that I want her to come home for an important assignment."

# CHAPTER TWENTY-ONE

## Overfull Gutters

On a Thursday in winter, Biase's home government approached her. They urged her to come home and help in finding a solution to the perennial crises in her country. They followed up on the invitation through her country's embassy in USA. The indignity created by violence in her country was worrisome but not new to Biase. She was only surprised and impressed that they found her.

She took a deep breath and talked to herself, "Nothing shall disturb your peace, I declare! We will not allow it."

Gently shutting the door, she caught a glimpse of her laptop and figured it beckoned at her. Then she called out to her husband.

"Lande, please come over and see this mail." Her husband stooped over her shoulder, peering into the laptop.

"What? Are they asking that you quit your UN job and go over to Nigeria to stay?" Her husband was alarmed at the thought of it.

"That's what it's sounding like. I am confused, Lande, what do you think?"

"That's nonsense. How can they ask you to…" Lande flared.

Biase stared at him.

Silence.

Lande appeared to have been struck by sudden dumbness.

"Yes, it's national duty alright but my family counts too," he spoke again, with a lingering frown.

"I reckon that keeping my job while our people suffered amounts to selfishness and lack of patriotism but then leaving my family to go for this assignment could mean abdicating my domestic responsibility, my family succour. Darling, this is where I need you most, now. Please what do you think? Perhaps I could go with the children. But then what about you? Oh my God! My head is breaking."

Faced down, she held her head with her two hands. Lande looked at his wife, not exactly knowing who needed more help.

Silence again, this time, longer. Lande battled several issues in his mind, changing from placing his cheek in his palm to heaving sighs. At last he spoke.

"Okay. I understand what you mean. I feel your dilemma. Yes, we must put heads together and try and reach a compromise but that will be some other time. I need a break." Troubled, Lande stepped outside, as if to get some fresh air and sunshine. He reclined on their outdoor couch, letting his hands drop by his sides. Biase, still struggling with dilemma, shut down the laptop and went to lay her heavy head on a pillow and stretched her weary body and legs on a bed. It took one long week for Lande and Biase to come out of their low spirits.

"Biase, you know what?"

"What?"

"You could actually ask for a leave of absence and relocate to Nigeria for this duty and probably come back when you have completed the national assignment."

"Wow! Lande! Are you for real?"

"And if your request is granted," he put his hand across his chest, "I promise to man the home solely."

Biase was jumping and clapping now.

"Hey, everybody come and meet the sweetest husband in the whole wide world. Thanks, darling." She jumped on Lande, heaving a huge sigh of relief and hugging him. Biase called Lande all the sweet names that came up in her mind and lavished him with sweet pecks.

Lande spoke again.

"Let's see how it goes. I am even looking beyond that."

Lande too figured that he could use the same opportunity to go home and explore the possibilities of setting up an information technology concern, considering that his country was still backward in terms of computer technology and cybernetics. The letter Biase received through an express surface mail with government seal said that all expenses were going to be paid, for the whole family to relocate, and Lande thought that was a great opportunity for the entire family to visit and feel part of home. He imagined how pleased their parents and relations would feel, not only seeing their children and grandchildren but also spending some good time with them. He also obtained a leave of absence from his workplace after his wife had received hers and they both planned the movement.

Three months after the initial government contact was made, the Dagamas returned to Nigeria and settled in Lagos, where integration processes began. The children were enrolled in good schools and Lande started making gradual headway in the emerging business terrain of information technology. Biase also made remarkable progress on the task for which she came home, taking it step by step, and gathering information. The leave of absence now appeared to hang in the balance, as home got real sweet to them. They found it amazing that they were beginning to prefer home to anywhere else, in spite of some of the regular challenges they faced. They were surprised to find out that the challenges were not insurmountable after all.

Leaning as usual on the balcony railing upstairs one morning, chatting and looking beyond the wall that fenced the compound, Lande and Biase unconsciously watched the movements on the street.

"Hello there, welcome to the neighbourhood," an elderly man strolling down the street waved at them, raising his eyes and squinting to look at them.

"Hi, good morning sir. How are you doing?" Biase responded.

"Can I come in?"

"Sure, why not." Lande went downstairs and let the man in. They shook hands.

"Kole is the name. I am a retired civil servant," and looking up, "is that your wife?" he asked

"Oh yes, that's my wife. Come in."

They both went upstairs and joined Biase at the balcony.

"Hello madam, my name is Kole Simpson. I live down the road. I was just taking a walk when I saw you both. I know you are new in this neighbourhood, that's why I decided to call on you. If you desire more information about the area, I can be of help. I have lived here long enough to be able to talk authoritatively about this area. I retired from the Railways two years ago."

"Welcome, sir. Please take a seat," Biase said and withdrew to the house. She came back with snacks and drinks and they all sat round a table to snack and chat.

"Railways? A lot of daddies worked there. Must have been an interesting place to work."

"It was in those days, but when our people took over, things spoiled. Do you know that I have not been paid even a farthing since I retired?"

"What? How have you been carrying on then?" Lande was surprised.

"Well, I managed to save up money and put up a building, in my active days. I live there with my wife and I have some tenants who pay me rent. I guess I am lucky; most of my counterparts are gone."

"How about the rest of your family?"

"Our children are all on their own. They come to see us from time to time."

"So why have you not been paid after your retirement?" Lande pried further.

"I think the government should be in a better position to answer that question. They said something ranging from no money, to a large number of retirees, but I think it is all about poor planning and inefficient management. The challenge of retirees is just one of the numerous troubles government has not been able to take care of."

The retiree seemed to have said it all and there was silence. Looking exhausted, he took a bite of his snack while Biase looked on. Lande's eyes caught a small bundle of long plank strips and some green coloured soft gauze, carefully packed near the flower bed, within the compound. Then he turned to his wife, pointing at the bundle of plank.

"That carpenter should have completed the gauzing of the windows and doors by now so we can lock those enemies out." His wife looked at him, unable to connect immediately.

"I mean the mosquitoes or are they not enemies?"

"Oh, of course they are."

"Fixing door and window gauzes would reduce considerably the occurrence of malaria caused by the enemies. Wouldn't it?"

"That way, our children's health would be better guaranteed. We indeed need to fix the gauze fast," Biase replied.

"Of course, it would prevent mosquitoes from entering your home. If I had been this savvy, I probably would not have lost two of my children to malaria, in those days. Quite regrettable," Mr. Simpson's voice dropped.

"Oh, sorry about that sir."

"Thanks. It's okay but quite regrettable because it was avoidable. What you are doing is the correct thing to do." Mr. Simpson tried not to be moody.

"But frankly, I feel for the teeming population out there who cannot afford to gauze their windows and doors? Lande added.

"Yes, so unfortunate," Biase said. "Sure you remember last week when we went visiting?"

Lande nodded.

"You saw those stinking, stagnant, putrid overfull gutters?"

Lande nodded again.

"That's where they breed, the mosquitoes, the enemies. But the people they bite do not help matters either. They throw all sorts of things into the gutters. That day, I saw a dead rat in the gutters. I also saw cellophane and nylon, broken bottles, cans and leftover food in the gutters. It is worrisome. The sorry thing is that by the time we got to the end of the street, I noticed that the gutters were not channeled anywhere. They were mere long shallow pits. And you know what? The windows were not gauzed and doors of the people in most cases were open, right next to the open gutters. Low windows without net." Biase sounded sad.

"Yes, my dear. I remember seeing you near tears on that day. That was in Aguda, Surulere. We were on a condolence visit. I think the various governments should be more responsive and channel gutters somewhere, say into the canals, so that the contents can flow. Also, gutters do not have to be open, some slab over them would make a healthy difference. Governments must also continue to educate the masses on how not to throw rubbish into gutters. Also mosquitoes must not be allowed to breed and increase otherwise you know what that means for the teeming population of humans."

"I know," Lande concurred.

"Incidentally, the government is aware of this," the old man seemed sure of what he was saying. "It was recently in the news that they are embarking on huge channelisation works to help clear the heaviness and beautify the environment."

"That's good, we are waiting." Lande hoped but the old man was not done yet.

"I think though that as that goes on, something should also be done to enable us citizens save money on the petrol and diesel we use for alternative power generation."

"Exactly," agreed Lande.

"It is incredible that through personal capacity, more electric power is generated from alternative power supply than from the central source of supply, the national grid. Amazingly, everybody is now used to the noise from the generators. It has become normal," Mr. Simpson paused and alternated a brief but definite gaze between Lande and Biase, and continued, "You, and perhaps I, can afford this alternative but there are many who cannot. What becomes of them?"

"It boils down to the same concern. The government at all levels must be more responsive and sensitive to the people's distress over electric power supply, bad roads, worrisome education and health systems, unemployment and indeed, several others. Sure these have burdened the people a great deal."

"I agree with you. I get scared when I see the number of unemployed youth hovering around town. I fear that they can easily be used as tools for destruction. They could be an important factor in the perennial insurgence that has given Mr. President sleepless nights," Biase let out, tickling the old man's imagination.

"Sleepless nights? The President? How did you know that?"

"Oh no, nothing special. Just what we pick up from the news every day. Is it not natural that the President should get worried over these issues?"

"But is he? Are they?"

"I think he is, he just has to be," Lande replied. Silence ensued for a short while, only to be broken by the old man.

"Okay o, if you say so."

"I say so, I even know so"

"You are such a nice couple. Where are the kids? I had seen them playing once when I passed by."

"Oh, they are in their room, sleeping. Thanks for your love, how nice of you," Lande said.

"You have been wonderful hosts. I appreciate my stay with you. Thanks for your company and the refreshment," Mr. Simpson said.

"It was a great pleasure having you with us. You are welcome to our home any time."

Lande accompanied him to the gate and came back to his wife.

"What an articulate old man!" Lande said.

"He still looks strong and alert, quite different from the traditional retiree."

"But why won't they pay them, for God's sake."

"You heard him, no money, too many retirees. He tried to find out what I meant by the perennial issues giving the President sleepless nights. I almost let the cat out of the bag and he was going to know more than was necessary."

"The issue about which the President invited you home?"

"Precisely!"

"Good he did not hear more but I see with you. If people are well educated and get employed or even if they are not that educated but have a steady income generating venture, perhaps low or mid income, they'd be otherwise occupied and have little or no time for truancy."

Lande moved closer to his wife as he spoke. He drew her close to him and kissed her. With his head rubbing on her forehead, said, his breath flowing directly unto her face, he said, "But we can talk about these issues some other time. Let's check on the kids."

He grabbed her by the hand and led her to the children's room.

# CHAPTER TWENTY-TWO

## The Specialist

Biase's people got wind of the progress she had made and were stunned; their hearts dulled with heavy apologetic feelings. Idiapa felt more haunted by the unfair treatment he meted out to Biase than that which he did to her parents.

"See how our poisoned fingers nearly got into our mouths?" one community elder, Maxwell, had remarked during one of their meetings.

"How?" The others retorted.

"First, we harassed the man into running away from home and meeting his death in the creeks, then the man's own brother chased away the man's only daughter, rendering her homeless. What poison could be more potent?" Elder Maxwell took them to task.

"Ohoo, Oyiga! May his soul continue to rest in peace!" Elder Makelu said with a sigh.

"Amen!" they all responded.

"At least we have twin boys from his wife. And his daughter, our daughter, is doing very well; so well that the Head of State has invited her to come and work for him." Elder Makelu always had information to share, just like elder Josomo.

"You mean it?" Elder Ozeh asked.

"You no read paper? You no look television? You no even hear radio?" Elder Jumuwa taunted, looking at Ozeh, who ignored him.

"Oh yes," Maxwell confirmed. "It's been on the news. The President invited her for an assignment and they are all back now. She is happily married to a progressive handsome young man from the next village and they have three great children. They came back together. Didn't you see them when they visited Naminsa?"

"No, I didn't. I had an urgent call from my in-laws so I went visiting them. But I was told. I would very much have loved to see them too. Oh! Oyiga's daughter."

"When I heard they were around, I went to Rita's house to see them. Rita's joy was so substantial; you could carry it in your arms. But I tell you, Idiapa could not find where to hide his face," Elder Maxwell said.

"I was not able to go and see them but I learnt that their three children look like and speak like oyibo. They too."

"Yes o, I saw with my eyes and, oh, I remembered everything. Naminsa should never repeat what it did to that family." Maxwell was full of regrets.

Biase had earlier held a meeting with the President and his Cabinet, in Abuja, with the States Protocol and the media present. The presidential protocol team received Biase and her husband at the airport and drove off with them after brief airport formalities. The couple truly enjoyed the ride in a fresh smelling tinted glass, latest model Mercedez Benz saloon car, convoyed in front and behind by two Toyota Camry cars each. They loved the beautiful scenery of Abuja, adorned with lofty mountains on many sides. On arrival, and without waste of time, it was straight to a press conference of sorts. Meeting room A of the presidential villa was filled with people from all walks of life, NGOs, rights groups, women's groups, youth groups, the military, the police, legislators and market groups. Everyone stood up when the President entered. He gesticulated to them with both hands signalling them to sit down. Cameramen feasted on Biase, with their shots, as she sat beside the President. It was like the camera click would never stop. Biase radiated with joy. The President began to address the audience, after welcoming them again. His chief press secretary had already welcomed and made them comfortable.

"I must confess that I am greatly burdened by this problem of citizens killing fellow citizens. People take delight in doing this, some claiming to be fighting for God, others because of unfounded hate or political and ethnic differences, while some do it just for the fun of it. There is no regard for precious human life and this gives me sleepless nights. Something just has to be done and sitting beside me here is a specialist to whom we look to help us find solutions to this problem. Mrs. Dagama has achieved success in other countries. We hope she will perform the same feat in her own country. Let us all welcome Mrs. Biase Dagama."

As the applause rent the air, Biase rose and took a bow.

"And of course, success is sweeter when shared with a spouse. I was reliably informed that Mrs. Dagama has enjoyed tremendous support from her husband, Mr. Lande Dagama, sitting right over there." The President gesticulated toward Lande and he rose to take a bow. Biase then got up to respond to the President's speech.

"Your Excellency, Ladies and Gentlemen," she placed her right palm on her chest and bowed slightly. "I'd like you to note that I feel greatly honoured by this invitation." She took her hand off her chest. "I thank Mr. President and all Nigerians for the trust reposed in me. I also thank my dear husband for his immense support. All I promise is that by the grace of God, I will do my utmost best not to betray the confidence you have reposed in me. I solicit your support, as I settle down to carry out this assignment. Please note that it is only with your support that I can have the enabling environment required for this task; and I want to believe that you will motivate and propel me to action."

There was pin-drop silence, broken only by Biase herself when she asked, "Sure I have your support, right?"

A thunderous "Yes" accompanied by loud applause came. After the meeting, security details whisked away Biase and husband to avoid exposure to unnecessary paparazzi and propaganda. They were driven back to the airport to catch the evening flight back to Lagos, from where she began her research. Biase's professional research method involved first finding the root cause of whatever issue she was tackling.

Disguised and looking quite ordinary, she got in the midst of the people, starting from a market in the Ojota area of Lagos.

"Madam, abeg I wan buy pepper. How much you dey sell am?" Biase approached a market woman.

"Twenty Naira dis one, fifty Naira de oder one."

"I also wan buy tomato, onions, egusi, crayfish and palm oil"

"Madam come sidon inside, sun too much"

The woman provided a plastic stool and Biase sat down while the woman packaged the ingredients.

"I jus come from abroad," Biase informed the woman.

"E show for your face," she replied without looking up, busy packaging the items Biase had requested.

"For there dem dey say small time our country go quiet, small time we go begin kill people, na true?"

The woman now paused and looked at Biase.

"Hmm, na true o, Madam but na de big big people dey cause am. My people say the bird wey dey dance for road, the ting wey dey givam music dey inside the bush wey dey near the road. You hear me so?" Biase nodded.

"Ah, but how you know say na di big oga dem dey cause am?"

"How I no go know? Who no know sef? Owl cry for night, pikin die for morning, who no sabi say na owl kill pikin? Abegi, me I don tire jare. Na dem. De big big oga dem."

"Eeheh! Okay, thank you customer. How much be my money?"

"One thousand three hundred Naira."

Biase paid and left with the ingredients. Still clutching the money she had just been paid, the informant, now spotting a smile, stood watching Biase make her way through the crowd. Biase got out of sight; the trader looked at the cash in her hand and heaved a sigh.

"Hmm, dis kain customer sef, God I thank you oh!" she muttered, looking up. Biase had several such informal interviews with people, and everybody seemed ready to talk. Everybody seemed fed up. Everybody was of the same opinion. All the questions she asked respondents and the requests she made from informants were tailored toward identifying the root cause of each of the problems identified.

Biase was struck by the sheer force of the teeming population.

Wherever she went, people swarmed and quite a number of them did not appear to have a clear-cut agenda. Able bodied men were seen under the tree or under some kind of shed, sitting or lying on long wooden forms not performing any specific function. Sometimes they were seen scooping into their mouths cooked rice and stew from time-beaten enamel bowls, a sign of a guaranteed one square meal. She saw adolescents, teens and youth roaming the streets, including children, some hawking items such as sachet water and running across roads, daring fast-moving vehicles, just to make a sale. Biase held her breadth when a vehicle screeched and a lad hawking peeled oranges escaped being crushed by a vehicle in high speed. Catching his breath after the lucky dash across the expressway, the lad cried for his crushed oranges and lamented the strokes of cane that awaited him on arrival home. Biase stood by the side and watched motorcycle riders move meandering as if they owned all roads. News about their imminent ban was already in the air. She stood under an overhead pedestrian bridge and watched pedestrians shun the bridge and dash across the busy expressway.

"Oh my God! Everybody appears to be king of the road here. Ha!"

She took a deep breath and exhaled. After several enquiries, she found it necessary to go to a nearby public transport motor park, in search of touts she could possibly have a chat with. She walked up to a mini shop and began to interact with the shop owner. The motor park turned out to be an eye opener.

"Madam, abeg give me any canned soft drink wey cold." She was truly thirsty.

"You wan sidon?" the woman was already dusting a stool. "O ya, wa joko." She invited her to take a seat, gesticulating towards the stool. A young man stood in one corner of the shop as if waiting for his turn.

"Yes o, I tire well well. Thank you." She sat down.

Biase observed the goings-on at the park. The shop had several bottles of highly alcoholic drinks and other edible stuff. Drivers came in and asked for shots of liquor which they gulped and then hopped behind the wheels, ready to take off with buses loaded with travellers. The touts were all over, spotting out travellers and leading them to waiting vehicles. One of them approached the mini shop where Biase was seated. His eyes were reddened, his hair granular, perhaps having had nothing to do with a comb for days. His body had a stale smell. His voice was cracked.

"Bros, give me that ting," he addressed the young man in the shop. The young man raised a heap and produced a wrapped substance, which he handed to the tout, who stretched out his hand as if asking for something else.

"Oh sorry, take, I don nearly forget." He gave him a lighter.

The tout unfolded the paper and spread out the content evenly. Then he carefully rolled the paper tightly around the substance. Biase watched the wrap turn to something like a thin cigarette. He lit the roll, inhaled and puffed out. The smoke encircled and dissipated. Left with no choice, Biase inhaled some of it. The tout threw the lighter at the young man and disappeared within the park.

"Madam, what does that mean?" Biase felt beaten.

"Shh! I no want trouble, abeg." The woman had turned her face away from the transaction between the tout and the young man. Biase turned her gaze toward the young man. Their eyes met and his cracked voice sounded.

"Madam, wetin be your mission sef? You never finish your drink?"

"I don finish. Madam, take your money." She paid and left the shop, heading toward another part of the park. She was now thinking about all she had seen.

"Hmm! Easy-to-reach human tools! Easy-to-access activating substance! This amounts to combat readiness!"

She gathered more information by asking questions and by observation within the motor park, before leaving the environment.

## CHAPTER TWENTY-THREE

# The Twins were Girls

Her findings at every point revealed, first of all, that every group and most people considered their own ethnic group and religion superior to the others. Every ethnic group had a derogatory name for the other and none hesitated in castigating the other. Her findings also uncovered the role played by the twin evil of religious indoctrination and bigotry. Also, the civil war that the country fought earlier had bred deep-seated hatred, which helped to fuel the crises or fan their flame. Yet another finding was a perceived inability of government to maintain balance and equity in the distribution of the nation's wealth. The winner takes all and get rich quick syndromes were also found to be strong factors. All these, together with several others, combined to form the background of her report and the starting point of her investigation. She laid bare these points as factors that could trigger regular unrest in her country. Armed with this fact, she compiled one section of her preliminary reports. She was soon to discover that the picture she got from her short stay in markets and motor parks was a vivid representation of happenings in all the other parts of the country she visited. She had earlier documented the chat she had with people at Abakaliki and Abonima, and the picture they painted of governmental neglect at the central level baffled her.

In the course of her investigation, during which time she travelled extensively within Nigeria, she discovered that the problem the country was faced with was indeed hydra-headed and required a lot of patience, sacrifice, and a great deal of tact to deal with. She found out that group membership was popular and that most of the groups had secret godfathers and sponsors, who used them to settle scores and achieve selfish aims. From her findings, a good number of the group members did not know exactly why they were in the groups. They were just there, ready to take orders to go forth and strike. Most of them were severely poverty-stricken and depended on the stipend per strike they were given. The strength of the stipend helped to keep them combat-ready. They were neither in schools nor at workplaces. Biase kept her ear to the ground and diligently recorded stories and life situations. Now in a village in Kaduna, she randomly interviewed women, men and youths. The villagers told her about a man whose children's attitude had brought about raised eyebrows in the community. Even while not quite sure what Biase was going to use the information for, they opened up to her, kind of reporting a certain man called Suliban to her. She had ealier approached Suliban for a brief chat and found him helplessly in need of listening ears. Biase was a bit surprised how come the small community of Samina had big chunks of information for her. Now certain that her previous discussion with Suliban was particularly revealing, she went back to him for a recap. The 39-year old bricklayer had told her during their first meeting, that he used to go from village to village to do his bricklaying job, for which he was paid little money, and regretted that people did not seem to be interested in building any longer. On Biase's prompting, the man told the story of his life.

"I miss my father a lot. I think things were better during his lifetime. Luckily, I do not pay house rent today; we live in his house, which became mine after his death. Without money in my pocket, how would I have paid house rent?"

Biase's eyes prompted Suliban to go on.

"My wife's kiosk has become empty but my children are my biggest headache. Now Kande, the eldest is almost 17 years old. Do you know that she just managed to come out of secondary school? She did not come out with any result. She is not engaged in any serious activity and I think she is getting fed up with her situation. Already she has joined the religious leader's assemblage, and there eh, people are told that only prayers, non-stop prayers would solve all problems. Would you believe that in spite of all that promise, the leader mingles with the females and forbids them from telling? We hear all these things. Kande never told anyone that the leader once got her pregnant and took her to Port Harcourt to terminate the pregnancy. But somehow we knew. She is always in need of money to take care of her toiletries and clothing. Unfortunately I could not provide that as often as she needed them but the village chief, from time to time, met that need in exchange of Kande's clandestine company. The secret leaked but the chief's four wives found out much later."

"How did you find out that your daughter went to Port Harcourt?"

"Walls have ears, you know, just take it that we found out."

"It is better to be very sure before talking. She may have gone for something else."

"Madam, please leave that thing. I know what I am talking about. After the race, you calculate the miles."

"How about your other children? You said they are your biggest headache. Apart from ehm…"

"Kande"

"Yes, Kande. So what about the others?"

"Uchenna, Kande's immediate junior sibling, dropped out of school just before hitting 15. As we speak, he fends for himself. He usually goes into the bush to gather wild nuts which he sold and pocketed the money from the sales. He hardly slept in the family house. He goes out and comes in whenever he likes; we don't have control over him. Oluranti, Uchena's immediate junior, is 14. He plays a lot but reluctantly helps out at home. He is always looking very rough and unkempt with scratches all over his often dry skin. Whenever he sets his eyes on money, whether mine or his mother's, he takes it. He does not perceive the act as stealing; he sees it as only taking. In a term, he might just be in school for a total of one month or so. He never came home with any school report. Each time I look at that boy, I feel sorry for myself."

"Let me interrupt you here, Suliban. Did you ask for his school report?"

"I am sorry, madam. I did not ask. Perhaps I failed there. But I had no money and was ashamed to ask him. I was not giving him money for school books so how can I ask him for school reports. That's why I look at him and feel shame."

He hissed, shook his head and added. "Madam, you won't understand."

"I understand everything you are saying. Trust me, I do. But go ahead."

"Ehen… their mother struggled daily in a dilapidated kiosk, praying that customers would come up and buy from her. Meanwhile her belly was getting bigger."

"She was pregnant?"

"Hmmm." Suliban nodded. "Me, I was expecting them to call me for building work, but no work."

"Hm, please go on."

"I have another son called Osaze. He is the quiet one, very obedient. Osaze is slightly above 12 years old but he is taller than Ranti, his elder brother. Sometimes Risna and I just could not help feeling that Osaze is the only child we have."

"That's your wife's name. Risna?"

"Yes, sorry I did not tell you. Quite often, Osaze helps his mother at the kiosk and at home. After Osaze, the next child is Garuba. This lad looks sickly and without much strength. No one bothered him because he was very frail. He went to the village school when he could. In that community, tuition was free and parents were only required to equip their children with school books, but only few parents did."

Suliban yawned and stretched himself.

"I'm so sorry Suliban, making you go through this."

"Nooo, I am happy to see someone who is interested in my story. No one cares here. We are just on our own. Who knows, you might even be of help to me and my family. Please, Madam, if there is any help you can render, I'll be grateful." Biase nodded.

"Okay, Suliban, but I am just wondering how possible it is for one man to be saddled with all these problems. It is incredible."

"I am here live telling you what happened to me and you are doubting me. Do you think I am fabricating stories? There are many of us with similar stories. I can take you to them. Life is not easy for us, although for some it is different. Please don't make me feel worse by disbelieving me. This is my true life story." Suliban seemed to have lost his equanimity, making Biase almost unsure of herself, at that point.

"Oh no Suliban, don't get me wrong. Please continue" Her eyes persuaded him. His breathing was deep.

Moments passed and he said, "She later had twins"

"Who had twins"?

"My wife."

"Hei! So sorry. Please tell me about your twins."

They came two years after Garuba.

"I am sure you stopped after the twins."

"The twins were girls. Anyway, we made a move to stop after listening to a group's talk about family planning and correct child spacing on radio."

"That was a good move. I hope you followed through."

"The religious leader's sermon one Sunday put my wife in a big dilemma. He had told his congregation that no human had the right to prevent conception because it is very sinful."

"So what happened next?" Biase was stirred up.

"They give him a lot of respect, so anything he says, that's what they do. Risna got pregnant again." Biase who had become very troubled by this time, figured that the pregnancy must have advanced without adequate nutrition and welfare but Suliban assured her that they carried on with hope. She also gathered that when the woman was due, she had a prolonged labour period and became too weak to push the baby out. Biase learnt that the community health centre where Suliban's wife went to have her baby could not handle the Caesarean Section which was recommended so she was transferred to the Teaching Hospital, first on a motorbike to the city where a cab could be found to transport her to the specialist hospital.

"The operation was successfully carried out," Suliban said to Biase, with a ray of hope. "Risna had four pints of screened blood. I was sitting right there, by her side when she woke up and gave me a smile. I smiled back and touched her forehead. I was happy."

"You were there."

"Yes. How are you? I asked her, thrilled to hear her voice. She nodded slowly, looking pale and weak. The nurses reported this situation to the Consultant Surgeon on ward round and he told them what to do."

"Take the vitals," He instructed.

"We just did, Doctor."

"Take it again."

One of the nurses complied and passed the jotting to the doctor, who placed his palm on Risna's brow, pressed open her eyes and looked into them and said to the patient.

"Open your mouth please."

"She did rather slowly." The doctor examined her mouth and asked her to jut out her tongue. He also checked it. He carefully touched her tommy, avoiding the plastered portion, then scribbled something on the folder.

"Watch her closely," the doctor said and moved over to another patient.

"So what happened next?"

"The nurses carefully administered the drugs and monitored the infusions and she soon fell asleep, even before I could tell her it was a boy. Unfortunately, Risna did not make it. She died at midnight and part of me died with her."

"Oh my God! What about the baby?

"He survived." Suliban lamented the death of his wife and at the same time, took it in its stride, adding, "God giveth and God taketh. What would be, would be. Perhaps that's the way God wants it." He blew his nose and returned the towelly handkerchief into the pocket of his trousers and looked at Biase with his misty eyes, as if to seek sympathy.

"So sorry about all that, Suliban."

He nodded and gave her a look of appreciation.

"I named my son Sunday to correspond with the day he was born. But the people, nicknamed the baby, Kwakashebu, meaning the one who kills."

Biase was speechless.

*The one who kills? How ignorant!* Biase thought to herself. And then said, "Eight children?" wondering what dire consequences the death of Suliban's wife had had on Suliban's family especially on baby

Sunday who was never breastfed. She kept moping at Suliban, who did not appear tired of talking.

"When this thing happened, my whole life just scattered. It was now Kande that was finally going to kill me. She had been pregnant and we did not know it. So she became a mother at 18, without knowing exactly who the father of her baby was. I had to take on the care of Kande's new born baby and Kande herself, financially and otherwise. With all the motherless…"

"Suliban, I think you need a break. You should stop talking and take a breather please."

"No, I am not tired. I want to talk. I want to…" Biase was surprised to see Suliban burst into tears. She called out to someone to bring some water. Suliban wiped his tears and blew his nose again with the same handkerchief. He bit open the tip of the sachet water and drank the whole of it. He bent over and remained silent for a while, then resumed talking.

Biase still had not found her voice, only wishing there was someone to help Suliban out with the rest of his story. Suliban told Biase that three years later, he married another woman who was bent on having her own children.

"Ah! This woman did not treat my other children as hers." He shook his head slowly, hissed and continued. "Life became more unbearable for all of us. Kande took her four year old daughter to her maternal grandmother and ran away to Abuja, where we were told that she became a prostitute. Reports came that Uche had joined some bad gangs operating at night, with arms along Lagos-Benin expressway. Madam, it was quite bad but at least they were fending for themselves. Ranti hawked wares on the traffic in Lagos. Osaze remained at home in Kaduna and was virtually converted to the new wife's slave. But he managed to pull through and is now a clerk at the local government office. Osaze is my only hope for now. Garuba died of malnutrition." Suliban planted a gaze on Biase. "You see my life?"

Biase thanked God that he did not after all feel completely hopeless.

"Hmm! What about the twins and the youngest one? They must have been very small."

"I took them to my late wife's mother, for assistance. For the love of her daughter, she took over the care of the children, even with no visible means of livelihood aside her mini crop farms. You know Kande's daughter was already there. One of the twins later died of measles while that last baby boy, Sunday, was struck with polio. Luckily, he was not completely paralysed. He only walks with a limp."

"Poor woman! How was she able to cope with the children?"

"Kande was sending money to her grandmother for the upkeep of her daughter but it could never be for her child alone. I also sent some money to my mother-in-law whenever I could. Kande stopped sending her money when she fell sick."

"Who fell sick? Kande or her grandmother?"

"My daughter became sick and we did not know what was wrong with her," Suliban told Biase it was later discovered that Kande contracted the HIV but did not find out in time. Whenever she travelled home from the city, she still went to see her church leader and the village head. Her ailment had not shown at the time. She had returned to the city and continued with her business. It took a long time for Kande to start feeling really ill but she still did not know what was wrong. Shuttling between the city and home, for herbal medication and prayers was now regular until she became very ill and could not shuttle anymore. At that point, she was hospitalised at the Teaching Hospital, where she eventually died."

"How sad, but how did you get to know that she was dating both the religious leader and the community chief?" Biase asked, overwhelmed with pity for Suliban.

"The walls have ears. The village chief became very sick. His last wife died but he appeared resistant although he succumbed after a while and died too. When the religious leader came down with the same symptoms, nobody was in doubt as to what the matter was. He was lucky that some non-governmental group discovered and placed him on medication. He is still there but it is like he is not there. Heavy scandal rocked the community church and more than half of the members left."

"This is a sad story, Mr. Suliban. I am so sorry about all that. But do your children contact you at all?"

"No, they don't. They are all masters to themselves. But like I hinted earlier, I am looking up to Osaze. He is the only one that contacts me."

Biase hissed, shaking her head slowly, her eyes closed. Silence. Then Biase spoke.

"It is indeed a pity that all these can happen to only one man. It looks and sounds unbelievable but sitting here, looking at you and listening to your story, I have no cause to doubt you."

"It is true. Everything I told you happened the way I said it."

"But what made you trust me so much as to confide in me and tell me everything?"

"Madam, you had earlier told me that you are on a research mission from the UN. I am quite educated, my father sent me to school. Never mind that the troubles of life placed me in such a pitiable state but I have faith in God that I will bounce back. I am educated so I know what it means to research on an issue. Lies will compromise research results. Besides, who knows, you might be in a position to help me some time in the future. I need help."

"I know Suliban. Let's just keep our fingers crossed." She opened her hand bag and brought out some money. "Here!" She called his attention and placed the money on a small table.

"Please send this to your mother in law, for the upkeep of the children in her care."

"Thank you, Madam. This is a lot of money. God bless you!"

"God bless you too, Mr. Suliban," Biase replied and adjusted herself on the seat.

"Before I leave Mr. Suliban, I'd like to know if you'd be willing to be part of my assignment. I am narrowing down my research to religious and ethnic riots and killings in the country."

The glow in his face betrayed his willingness to assist. And Biase asked further.

"How much about these do you know?"

"They are intertwined and somehow difficult to know which one is taking place at any point in time. Sometimes it looks like something that must happen but that is waiting for the right time."

"How?"

"Because it happens and we forget it and later it happens again and before long it happens again. It's scary."

"Who are those involved?"

"I don't know. But we can't rule out jobless youths who are manipulated by godfathers, who have a stake in the exercise. It does not take time to gather them. Their leader knows how to get about it whenever the need arises. And because they are jobless and are given a stipend each time they strike, they are always eager to strike."

"Can we identify them? Can you be of help? We'll pay for any service you render."

Suliban was pensive but nodded slowly more than once. Biase knew she would need him. She decided on the spot that she would give him some time, while her preparations went on.

"Okay, Mr. Suliban. I'll get back to you when I need you. I'll be on my way. Bye for now."

"Bye, Madam; thank you very much," Suliban replied, a broad smile dancing on his face.

Biase left, feeling that Suliban's household was a veritable nest of ready human tools and Suliban himself, a potential instrument of repair. Biase documented her findings again and was soon ready for another phase of her work, which would require her meeting the leaders and prominent members of all militant groups and factions.

"This no doubt is the most tasking of the assignment. My documented report is growing large but the individual characters that make up the document are at large. How and when can I talk and listen to people that will give me a practical dimension of my work?" She spoke to herself and thought about another meeting with Suliban.

"Madam, I already made a few contacts. We would need to travel widely for us to make headway.

"Further headway, you mean?"

"Yes. I will travel with a companion. Achoba is his name and he has a lot of ideas. If we are adequately mobilised, in a week's time, you'll have more than enough materials to work with."

"Don't worry about that. Invite as many as possible. Just remember that we are looking at militant groups and all factions. It is going to be like a meeting, seminar, training or even a conference. Also do not forget that I am on a research mission from the UN. I hold the olive branch."

"No problem!"

That now sorted out, Biase waited for Suliban and his companion while still interviewing others for more information.

# CHATER TWENTY-FOUR

## The Informants

Stunned by the depth of her discovery through Suliban and others, Biase settled at the Transcorp Hilton Hotel Abuja, where she lodged for the last lap of her assignment. She had suggested short and long term solutions as panacea, the short term action being what she was currently trying to do while the long term solution lay in the development of projects that would lift people out of poverty and hunger, and create opportunities for socio-economic empowerment, growth and development. This way the strikers would recognise the existence of such words as dignity, prestige, integrity and decency, and begin to identify with them. Also the method of upbringing must change and be devoid of impunity. Biase had found out that most parents knowingly or inadvertently instil the culture of impunity in their children by brazenly speaking and practising it. She remembered a young man had told her that his father used to say this to him: "Don't spare those cursed people, if they do any nonsense, just slit their throat and spill their useless blood!" Biase shuddered again at this thought and concluded that the level of ignorance that existed within the people was killing them. She had therefore recorded and recommended that at least basic primary education should be compulsory and non-negotiable irrespective of religious or cultural affiliations. Secondary education too, after primary education had been achieved. Biase had recommended also that meaningful focus should be placed on grassroots development as opposed to what she had noticed – neglect of the grassroots and focus on urban development. Her next task was not only to identify groups and their ring leaders but also to assess the strength and destructive capacity of each group. At this stage, she knew she had to hire more competent hands to assist her with the task of identifying more groups and getting them to come for dialogue. More funds for the mobilisation of respondents had been made available to facilitate her work. Her friend, Suliban, had been of great assistance in mobilising the groups which are spread all over the country. The other assistants did an equally good job. Among all the groups, which included the ethnic militia groups and militants, the ones she categorised as most broad-based and most dangerous were the groups that specialised in ethno-religious killings and as a result, the ones she would tackle first. Biase had ensured a widespread social research that involved several paid informants from different tribes and ethnic groups. Different groups existed, she was told, but that there were two main factions led by Bunkar and Shamar, two strong young men, dreaded and feared, commanding tremendous attention. She was told that they were very powerful, and all that Shamar in particular needed to do was to utter a word and it was carried out to the letter.

He had a hypnotic effect on his teeming followers. Shamar's gang was fingered as the trigger group that usually initiated action while Bunkar formed his own group to always counter Shamar's seemingly uncontrolled actions. Bunkar professed Christianity while Shamar had a firm belief in Islam. Bunkar had been brought up under close Christian supervision and had grown up to be a devout Christian who did not joke with his Christian beliefs. And Shamar, after engaging in an in-depth study of the two major holy books, arrived at the conclusion that the Koran was the final word from God and that the Christians were wasting their time with their bible. On his part, Bunkar concluded that no Moslem could go to heaven because they did not know the Way. Shamar had piously participated in several mayhems that destroyed the lives and property belonging to Christians, while Bunkar had always led his group to hit back in vengeance. Bunkar strongly believed that the only way to stop the insurgence of Shamar's group was to match fire with fire; so he got his group always ready for reprisal attacks on Moslems. It was deplorable indeed and seemed to have gone beyond governmental control, as innocent souls perished.

Biase who seemed to have succumbed to the task she had ahead, after a long puzzling day, let herself drop heavily into the hotel sofa, with a heavy sigh. From the information she got so far, she knew that she had an indeed huge job ahead. How would she tackle it? Where would she start from? Her head was full and tired, she dozed off on the sofa.

"I think the best way to start is to have separate chats with Shamar and Bunkar." Biase told herself when she got up. "It is important that I have frank chats with the key persons in each group, some of their key followers and friends, and if possible, their mentors. I also need to have talks with their parents but that will be later, after I have interacted with their offspring. I hope their parents are alive." Biase knew she had to prepare her mind for the task ahead. It was not possible for her to have access to those termed godfathers and mentors as hardly anyone agreed to point at the direction of the so-called godfathers. Biase did not necessarily have to speak with everyone invited, if she adjudged it not necessary. She discharged those ones, after preliminary talks and carried on with the others, starting with the ring leaders of the ethno-religious strikers. Then she moved to their followers, one after the other. All participants were lodged at the prestigious Transcorp Hilton, a move which thrilled them in such a way that they never stopped looking around in admiration of the whole environment. The next step was a motivational meeting which they had with Biase and some officials of the Presidency. Biase had already lodged there for some days, setting the stage for what she called the big project. Travel, lodging and feeding expenses of all invitees had been prepaid by the government and the invitees were made very comfortable. All participants were given their full allowances, including enough money to take them home. Some were happy at what they described as an opportunity to *chop* free government money. A short note placed in each of their rooms welcomed them to an opportunity to speak for others and urged them to be frank in whatever contributions they would make, for the benefit of all. Both Bunkar and Shamar were frank in speaking with Biase but Shamar's initial resistance was quite evident. As Biase had separate one-on-one meetings with Shamar, Bunkar, their parents and all the group members, Shamar viewed Biase with disrespect and gave an impression of being forced to come for the meeting and of not having time to waste. The signal Biase got from him was of 'hey woman hurry up', but Biase played along.

"Young man, please sit down. I'll not take much of your time, okay? I'll be brief." He sat down and Biase gave him a big smile and a 'thank you', and continued.

"I know you are Shamar. I want to let you know that government recognises you as someone who can help solve some of its problems. That's why you have been invited. So, congratulations!"

Shamar's lips curved in a suppressed smile and from that point, he became less turgid and their chat flowed.

"I'll ask you straightforward questions and hope to receive frank answers." Shamar planted his eyes on Biase. "I know you are a Moslem who has to share the same environment with Christians." Shamar nodded and Biase continued. "You also know that both religions preach peace, love and tolerance."

Shamar kept quiet.

"So why do you indulge in violence and killing?"

No answer. Biase let him be, satisfied with the result of the feelers she let out.

"Thank you, Shamar. That will be all for now. When next we meet, I hope you will be willing to at least say something to me."

He nodded.

"Alright, you may leave now."

Shamar stormed out of the room. Biase spent some time reflecting on the young man called Shamar and imagining what tough time she would have with him.

"Please ask the next young man to come in. His name is Bunkar." Biase's voice sounded on the phone.

Face-to-face with Bunkar, Biase wanted to know why he took it upon himself to lead reprisal groups.

"They think we are fools and want us to sit and watch them slaughter us like rams. Whenever we balance the power, they retreat."

"You speak good English. What's your educational level?"

"I am a Polytechnic undergraduate, studying Geology."

"So why don't you focus on your studies and leave violence. Who is your sponsor?"

No answer.

"You were talking about balance of power. Don't the scriptures say that vengeance belongs to God?"

Again, no answer. Bunkar only looked at Biase, with an obvious frown. There was silence. Biase broke it.

"But you know that you have to stop forthwith because it does not do anyone any good. If you see everybody as your brother or sister, you will find it difficult to harm them. Do you agree?"

He shrugged his shoulders.

"Why don't you say that to the other group? It takes two to tango. If I see you as my brother and you don't see me as yours, what's the use?"

Biase ignored his comment and continued to speak to him.

"I'd like you to. I ask you to stop violence, okay?

"Okay ma'am!" He breathed, raising his voice slightly, as if seeking an end to the questioning.

"Are my questions embarrassing you?" Biase teased.

"Not exactly ma'am, as long as they are not one-sided. We must not fold our arms and watch them kill us just like that. They too deserve to die. And whenever we hit back, they flee like cowards. They perhaps think that their lives are dearer to them than ours, to us. I am not embarrassed but the truth has to be said."

"I'll talk to you further, later. You may leave now," Biase said, as if in a hurry to discharge him.

"Thank you ma'am." He left, leaving Biase to wonder deeper about her amazing assignment.

Biase put across the same questions to the other young men separately and received a melee of contributions. Talking with so many youths was very tasking but Biase discovered one major thing: the boys were in dire need of home warmth, love, care and parental touch. In wondering why they lacked this touch, her thoughts flashed across to the Suliban family. She just imagined how far a gentle parental touch could go and regretted that it was lacking in many homes. She remembered her own past, particularly her uncle's wickedness to her and his wife's coldness. She found herself blessing and praising the Raboni

Sisters. The boys were reacting in response to certain stiff religious injunctions and beliefs, coupled with political inclinations, enabled by their low poverty-driven status. She found out that only a few of them were driven by ideology and not poverty.

"Hmm, their beliefs and inclinations are fuelled greatly by their respected spiritual and political leaders, under whose tutelage they have been and whose identity they have refused to disclose. They are not denying the availabilty of satisfactory remunerations and promises of political positions, which help to motivate them." Biase deduced as she spoke to herself, her fingers quite deft on the laptop keyboard, dexterously noting and documenting what the boys said. It took quite some time but she spoke with all invited.

# CHAPTER TWENTY-FIVE

## Crime does not pay

On the hotel corridor, a group of youths chattered rather loudly. "It looks like that woman has magic in her. Imagine how she just arrested me with her eyes and I was telling her everything," one of the group members said.

"You sure say no be because of the big pocket money wey dem give you na hin make you dey talk like that?" another replied.

"I no think so o. Ah ah, I never see money before? Na the woman joor. She get one kind style wey dey make person no fit lie."

"Wetin she ask you sef?"

"She ask me say which role I dey play for Bunkar group? Na im I tell am say I be hit man for that group, any time when dem do us and we want do dem back, I dey follow carry gun. Una know nah."

"E good to tell am truth, me sef I no lie for am"

"Shebi dem talk say dem wan stop the wahala? Eheen! I tell am say our own be say we no go strike first, but if dem strike, we go strike back. Dat na de truth and notin but the truth. Abi no be so dem dey talk am?"

The laughter that followed was quite boisterous. Just then, a door opened and a confused Suliban, who had been eavesdropping on the boys' conversation right from his room, peeped and muttered to himself.

"Is that not Uche's voice I have been hearing from inside this room?" Alarmed, he stepped out and sighting his son, shouted.

"Uche, what are you doing here?"

The young man was so stunned he almost melted, and could not utter a word, but it was actually like he froze on the spot, in the real sense of it. He opened his mouth and eyes and looked around at his friends and said rather emotionally, "He's my daddy," pointing soberly at Suliban.

"What are you doing here, Uche? So you are one of them eh? Oh my God, Uche." His father had his two hands on his head. As he fought threatening tears, the boys began to move away from the scene, returning to their separate rooms, leaving Uche and his father alone standing there.

Devastated, Suliban turned and made for his room. Uche followed him.

"Daddy, I have changed; the woman has changed me." He was kneeling now. "I am sorry. I'm sorry daddy." Uche sobbed and his father let out his own tears.

"Son, stop crying." Suliban quickly got his son up and pulled him close for a tight hug, saying to him, "I am sorry too; I did not take good care of you. You grew on your own." He was sobbing more profusely now. "I was poor and had many of you. There was not enough to go round and not much I could do. I am sorry, son. Oh Risna, where are you? I wish you were alive. Oh, Oh. Oh!"

"Daddy it's okay. Things will get better; in fact they are getting better. Thank God for this exercise, thank God for that woman!" Father and son sat down to frank talks and Uche made confessions to his father about the kind of life he led after leaving home and how on several occasions he had escaped being killed. Suliban had earlier heard that his son was an armed robber but the young man now confessed the details and left his father in no doubt that the young man had turned sober. They relived their past and nursed their wounds together, and Suliban felt better after, Uche too.

"Let's go and see Mrs. Dagama."

"Daddy, you know the woman? How did you know her?"

"Fate brought us together. She was in our home and we talked. She is on a peace mission, hired from the United Nations and had to draft me into her working group. I have worked with her since then."

"United Nations? She was in our house? Who brought her to our house?"

"I told you. Fate. God moves in a mysterious way, His wonders to perform." Suliban knocked on Biase's door.

"Come in!"

"Mr. Suliban, any information or something? Anything new?" Biase asked as father and son entered.

"This is my son." He pointed at Uche.

"Your son? Young man, are you not one of those I had a chat with just recently?"

"Madam, my son is one of them. Remember the Uche I talked to you about?"

"Yes, yes, Uche, the one…"

"Who joined the highway gang operating nocturnally. That's him but he just told me that you have changed him. He appreciates everything. Thanks be to God."

"Thank you, ma," Uche bowed as he spoke.

"You are welcome, son. I am glad you confess change. I hope you are truly a changed young man."

He nodded.

"Endeavour to remain so, okay? Crime does not pay."

"Yes, ma. Thank you, ma."

"Mr. Suliban, we'll talk more. Go and bond further with your son. It is very important." Biase watched them leave, savouring their reunion.

# CHAPTER TWENTY-SIX

# All Humans, God's Creation

"My dear wife, see me o! Our President don invite me for meeting. Who be me nah wey President dey invite me. See the letter," Bunkar's mother peeped into the letter and went back to her seat.

"Which kain meeting be that? Country dey spoil, dem dey give you letter. E fit be say na tea una dey go drink there."

"No be tea o. Na de country wey dey spoil na hin dem wan talk about for the meeting. Na so dem write am for the letter. Me I dey wonder why e come be me wey dem call. I hope say notin bad dey inside."

"Bad like how? Say you thief or kill person? Abeg make you just go, notin bad go dey there."

"Okay nah, I go go see as e go be."

It was Sharma's father's friend that took him up on his own invitation.

"My friend, you don join important people o. See nah, Presido invite you. I jealous you small o!"

"Na so I see am o, my brother. I just sidon dem carry letter come give me. I fear small o but the government person wey bring the letter say make I no fear, say dem want make we talk about some problem wey dey for Nigeria. See me nah, wetin I sabi wey I go talk. I go go sha."

"I sure say better reason dey wey make dem call you."

"Me sef, I think so."

It was quite understandable that the two men safeguarded their letters of invitation and made sure they went with the letters. They were also lodged at the prestigious Hilton, to their utmost amazement. It was the first time in their lives they got close to a place like the Hilton, let alone being lodged in it. The marvel was still all over them when Biase called Room Service for tea, during their initial meeting. The tea arrived and Bunkar's father wondered if his wife had become a prophetess.

"Please serve yourselves. Feel free and let's make it a tea meeting." Biase said, lifting the cover on a full tray' "What do we have here? Uh! Meatpie and sausage rolls, assorted tea, coffee, chocolate drinks, milk and sugar, including natural honey. Hmm!" She picked one roll, placed it in a saucer and poured some coffee into a mug, urging the men to follow suit.

Trying harder to warm up to them and relax their mood, Biase continued, "Hey! Go ahead, join me. Let's eat." She took a bite and cast a glance at them.

They managed to join her.

"Gentlemen, I welcome you most heartily. Try and make yourselves comfortable. I am Biase Dagama, Conflict Resolution expert from the United Nations. You see, I have introduced myself. Now let's know you more."

"My name is Mr. Yamua," Bunkar's father was the first to speak. Biase looked at the other man.

"Mr. Tonzaka," he said.

Biase adjusted her seat, cleared her throat and began to address them further. "Gentlemen, you must have heard the adage that says that the toad does not run in broad daylight for nothing."

They both looked at her without saying a word.

"The President has good reasons for inviting you for this all-important meeting."

"Where him dey? Him go come?" Tonzaka, Shamar's father asked.

Biase smiled.

"The President is not going to be here. I am representing him."

"You?" they both asked, not quite hiding their disappointment.

"Yes, gentlemen. He hired me from America to come and do a job for him and you have been selected to help me do the job and achieve results. I am sure you'll be willing to help me."

"How the work be?" Shamar's father asked.

"It is a *fix Nigeria* kind of work. You will agree with me that the level of violence in this country is too high. There are recurrent riots and counter riots, too much killing, maiming, burning, bombing. What should we do to stop the chaos?"

"Ah ah, Madam but why una invite me? I no know anything about riot nah," Shamar's father protested, followed by Yamua, Bunkar's father.

"Me too. Why you come invite me sef?"

"Your children are the ring leaders who spear head the riots. They call themselves Shamar and Bunkar. What do you have to say?"

"My son? Ring leader?" Shamar's father asked.

"Not my son o! How can my son be a ring leader?" retorted Bunkar's father, shaking his head fiercely. "Who told you? How did you know?" he added.

"Yes, how you know?" Shamar's father also queried.

Biase shocked them to the marrow when she told them that their sons had already admitted that they were the ring leaders.

"I have spoken with them."

"How?" they chorused. "We go fit talk with…?"

"Yes, at the appropriate time, after you have answered my questions."

She had already developed her questions but had to first intimate them with the serious matter on ground. They looked at each other and focused their gaze at Biase. The look in their eyes was between shock and hate. Biase sensed it but relaxed, on remembering that security operatives had been planted all over the hotel. She asked random questions like: *Are your sons living with you? Are they married? How come you did not know their whereabouts? How often do you stay together? Do they eat in your house or elsewhere?* These questions got them wondering, stammering and shaking, in a bid to answer them. And when Biase told them that their sons were actually being questioned for leading all the violent operations and counter-operations that have left the country in a chaotic situation, the men appeared broken. Biase noticed that the two men were devastated by the knowledge of their sons' involvement and needed to be stabilised before they could take any more questions. She remained silent and simply observed them for a short while. One of them opened his mouth and actually left it open with his two arms on his head, while the other one panted as if he would soon breathe his last. Droplets of sweat made their way from their face in the air-conditioned room.

"Easy, gentlemen. We'll sort it all out. This is simply the moment of reality and all I require from you is the truth. You'll have to tell me all you know; that's the only way we can make progress." Biase picked up the phone and called for some water. Minutes later, the men had each gulped two glasses of water. The man with his hands on his head now had both arms folded across his chest. He was pacing up and down while the panting man sat face down. They both were now less tensed up. Biase resumed her questioning. The demographic questions were the ones that revealed more and helped her overall understanding of the issues. Biase had fashioned the questions in such a way that they gave no room for falsehood. She documented separately everything said by both parents and as the meeting progressed, it became clear to her that youth or adolescence related challenges were more easily addressed when the assistance of the parents concerned is sought. She got them conscious of the magnitude of the problem and, anxious to find solutions, tapped into their adult memory. They wanted to get the embarrassing situation off their hands. Both parents made very revealing statements that provided useful information which Biase stored in her mind and recorded. Each of the parents talked about the circumstances surrounding the growing up days of his son and how much he loved him. None of them could explain how and at what point their children turned dissidents. Within an hour of interaction, Biase had scratched out all the basic information she required. And then it was time to get the two young men together with Biase. As they stood before her, she recalled all what their parents had earlier told her. The jigsaw began to fix itself and, as it did, Biase saw clearer pictures gradually emerge, revealing issues she had failed to figure out when she talked with them individually. She stared at them and their presence seemed to have suddenly scared her. But her professionalism always preempted and took care of situations that could get her scared for any reason. She quickly braced up, shook her head and reassured herself.

Whatever power they possessed threatened to make her shiver and feel like her heart would soon stop beating. *Are they going to attack me?* she wondered, still trying to conquer her fear and prepare to ward off any attack. It was as if a spell was cast on her and she was not quite sure what was happening. Her head spun when she looked at the boys and saw what she thought was a 'serves you right' look in their eyes. "They are poised to harm me, no doubt," she imagined but the young men themselves had become consumed by confusion and surprise. Biase soon got herself together and, angry at what she imagined, decided to be sterner with them, just in case they had plans to disrupt her work. The young men had noticed that the change in her demeanour was remarkably different from what they experienced during their individual visits when the woman received each of them. That was the first time the young men were standing side by side in one room. Biase thanked her stars it did not get to that.

"Gentlemen, please take your seat. Sorry about all that. By the way, did any one of you enjoy all that drama?" The confused men moped at her. "Are you both okay?" She asked.

"I am fine," replied Bunkar. Shamar simply nodded.

"Very well then, let's go." For formality's sake, she asked them the same questions she had asked their parents earlier, so as to achieve concurrence. She was pleased with the level of uniformity she achieved from the in-depth interview she had with the young men. Then she tried to find out more about why they found it necessary to always cause commotion. As they talked, Biase painstakingly separated chaff from grain, noting that it all boiled down to religious intolerance and superiority complex, absence of a solid state welfare system, and a muddled-up political system, characterised by misrule. She gave them a short sermon on the sameness, omnipotence, omnipresence and omniscience of God and told them that God was capable of sorting issues and definitely better than they would do. She gave them the antidote to the destructive urge that rose in them from time to time, painting pictures that affirmed that all humans were God's creation.

"When you kill, you are actually destroying the Creator's property and your fellow human being. Have you ever given a thought to the mystery of conception? Do you ever imagine how it eventually metamorphoses into the birth of a human being?" They stared at her as if she was a spectacle. "You are not and cannot be in control of this mystery. So how can you possibly want to control the life of a fellow human being resulting from this mystery, and even decide when to cut it short? Ah ah! Even God is saddened by your behaviour."

They just moped at her.

"One's religion," she continued, "could be termed an accident of birth because the religion you began with and assumed from childhood was the religion of your parents. So," she was now pointing at both of them, "either of you could have been son to either of your fathers. And in that case, you would have assumed the religion of the one who became your father. You would also have acclaimed the superiority of his religion over the one you are presently upholding."

The young men, uncomfortable, looked on as she spoke.

"It is on record," she continued, "that most parents do not even know that their children are the perpetrators of this evil. I call it evil because it is nothing but evil and you and your groups must begin to see it as evil and also see those that dwell in it as evil. Remember, evil does no one any good. Instead, it brings disrepute and dishonour. See how you have caused your parents to be *dragged* out of the comfort of their homes for questioning. They both expressed surprise that you have your hands in such embarrassing acts; you soaked your hands in human blood." She paused and gave them a disarming smile. They did not smile back. And then she added.

"I think that henceforth the parents of riot ring leaders will be detained and interrogated. I'll make that recommendation to the Presidency." She smiled again and added, "If you love and respect your parents, I am sure you will not want to see them embarrassed that way." The young men received that banter with a strange combination of grinning and frowning."

Biase hoped they understood that it was all in a lighter mood but as far as she was concerned anyway, she wished it could happen that way. She was not done yet.

"Do you agree with what I am saying?"

The young men nodded.

"So what's the point in killing for religious reasons or any reason at all? Why do you soil your hands?" Biase asked, adding that the destruction that trailed the crises they always spearheaded helped to deepen the underdevelopment level of the country.

"In the final analysis, you have not achieved anything," she charged, "except perhaps you have become horror champions of underdevelopment because your country can never be developed that way." By the time Biase finished, they had their gazes fixed on the ground and could not look her in the face. They too had been gripped by a strong force, an inexplicable crippling power that seemed to have rendered them limp. They did not know what hit them but were convinced that it was not ordinary. The session ended and the young men were expected to leave but they sat on, unable to figure out what their counsellor had done to them. Biase observed them, wondering why they ever allowed themselves to be used as agents of destruction. She sympathised greatly with their parents and wished that the godfathers could be fished out. One after the other, the young men sighed, hissed and yawned; one of them coughing and the other sneezing. Shamar stood up, followed by Bunkar. Heads bowed, they muttered their gratitude.

"Thank you, ma."

They both made for the door but Biase called out to them.

"Hey, won't you give each other a handshake? That'll be a good idea, you know."

The two men shook hands as if being forced to be friends and left while Biase sat back to review and process all that she had recorded. As she watched them move out, she felt she was not quite at peace with herself. "Is it because the job is in Nigeria and the culprits Nigerians?" she asked herself.

Biase ended discussions with all other invitees and extracted all the information she required, before dismissing them. Her searchlight was now focused on four main characters.

# CHAPTER TWENTY-SEVEN

## Crossing the T's and Dotting the I's

Biase sat face-to-face in the same forum with the fathers of the two ring leaders and the ring leaders themselves. It was no longer news that their names were all on the invitation list. Over the period of their stay, they had familiarised themselves with goings-on within the cozy environment. While Tonzaka and Yamua walked in together, Sharma and Bunkar came in at separate times. Biase's ever-ready smile welcomed them all to the forum. She began by asking those professional questions that tended to cross all T's and dot all I's and which have the potential of finally nailing the culprit.

"Gentlemen, I welcome you and plead that we all see this meeting as a friendly one because having been together for some days now, we should be seeing ourselves as friends. So far we have been frank with one another and I expect it to continue that way." She adjusted her seat and looked at them one by one.

"Please feel free to talk earnestly about your sons. We are all here for the same purpose, and that is, to save them and other youths from the mess they are in. There is nothing more to hide. That is why we are all here together. Luckily, your sons have admitted their wrongdoing."

The two men nodded. Their sons looked on. Biase noticed that the presence of the parents of these boys, courtesy of the Presidency, instilled a measure of fear, seriousness and soberness in the young men. She directed the first question to Shamar's father, Mr. Tonzaka.

"Sir, we have been told that you are the father of Shamar but I want to confirm it from you and in the presence of Shamar. Are you Shamar's father?"

"I am Shamar's father"

"Thank you," Biase said and turned to his son. "Shamar, is this man your father?" pointing at Tonzaka.

"Yes madam, he is my father."

"Good." She turned to Bunkar. "Is this other man sitting over there your father?"

"Yes, ma'am. He is my daddy."

Biase nodded and looked at Yamua. "Sir, this young man says you are his daddy, is that correct?"

"Correct, Madam," Yamua responded.

"Great! We are on track."

"Now Mr. Tonzaka, what can you frankly tell us about your son, Shamar?"

"All I will say to you is that my wife and I love this boy a great deal. He has been a stubborn lad but we did our best to provide and care for him and also correct his lapses but sometimes he gets beyond our control. On some occasions, he ran away from home and returned when he wished but we still love him a lot, in spite of all that."

Shamar remained silent as a frown lingered on his face. Bunkar gazed at him, expressionless.

"When you say he is a stubborn lad, what do you mean? Does he take drugs and alcohol? Does he womanise? Does he have too many male friends that may influence him? Does he even have too many female friends?"

"I am not sure his male friends can influence him o. Hmm! It can be easier the other way round. He does not smoke or drink but several girls flock around him. My wife and I persuaded him to settle with one of them, but to no avail."

"Settle with one of them? What about his education?"

"We tried to give him the best we could afford but he wouldn't just settle to his studies. Instead we noticed that he was becoming more interested in activism. We gave him a strict Islamic upbringing and he grew up to be a staunch Moslem but we are not happy with some of these fundamentalist traits we are hearing about. We are surprised."

"Did you try to stop him?"

"How do you catch a cloud and pin it down?"

This question sent Biase's mind to 'The Sound of Music', a film her husband brought home for their children which they always watched together and sang along as a family. In the movie, Reverend Sisters referred to restless Fraulein Maria and wondered if one could get her to stay in a place.

"So what is your occupation?" Biase resumed.

"I am a dealer in cement. I own a warehouse from where people make wholesale purchase. I also have a shop for retail sales."

"What does your wife do?"

"She is a full-time housewife."

"I see. Thank you, Mr. Tonzaka. We'll get to talk more, later."

Biase turned to Shamar. "Do you agree with him, Shamar?"

"I agree."

"You did not want to continue with your education instead you chose activism. Why?"

"Nothing, madam."

"Why did you not settle down with a wife as suggested by your parents?"

"I will soon get married."

"I pray!" his father interjected.

Biase gave Shamar's father a broad smile before turning to Mr. Yamua.

"What do you have to tell me, sir?"

Yamua spoke as Bunkar looked on.

"You see, Bunkar's mother and I are both carriers of the sickle cell gene." Bunkar had a surprise look on his face. "We did not know it. It was after all our three children died that someone advised us to go for a test. We did and discovered that we were both positive and that was why we lost the children. Devastated, we stayed on and licked our wounds. Today, thanks to God, we have two children. He looked at Bunkar and pointed at him. "Bunkar is one of them." Bunkar stirred in his seat.

"Thank God for that. Please continue"

"They both grew up under the watchful eyes of my wife and me. We are devout Christians, so we gave them a Christian upbringing." Yamua paused and looked at Biase and Tonzaka, who both nodded their eagerness to hear more.

"We later noticed that my boy was going out with strange peers and enjoying their company. We talked to him and he stopped moving with those boys. We never saw any of them in our house again. We heard about reprisal groups whose aim was to ensure counter-attacks so that aggressors will feel the pinch of their own aggression. I did not know initially that my son was a member, let alone being the leader of the group. By the time I got to know, he apparently had already gone far."

"Now that you are faced with the challenge how does it make you feel?"

"Surprised and sad. But he claims that the other group is scared of reprisals and that such counter-attacks made the aggressors think twice. He also claims that is the only way to put an end to recurrent insurgence."

"Balance of power. Some call it balance of terror. That's what it is but has it worked in this case?" Biase seemed to be talking to all but to none.

"I have now warned him to stop forthwith and he has promised to do so and also get his group members to follow suit," Bunkar's father said.

Biase turned towards Bunkar.

"Do you agree with all your dad said?"

"Yes ma'am, I agree. He is telling the truth."

"He is on drugs, isn't he?" Biase asked Bunkar's father.

"No. Far from it. I can vouch for him. He doesn't even smoke, neither does he drink. I brought him up with my own hands." He showed his hands. "I know him but you see, I can't vouch for his gang members and their influence over him."

"What's your occupation, sir?"

"I own a grocery store. We call it provision shop."

"And your wife?"

"She owns a fashion store which was looted and burnt during one of the riots. I think it must have been after that destruction that my son joined the reprisal group?" Bunkar nodded in agreement, the frown on his face speaking volumes.

"Thank you, sir. That would be all for now. More later." She turned to Bunkar again. "I ask you once more. You agree with everything he's said?" He nodded again.

"Very well then, please let's reconvene after lunch, say by 5.00 pm. Is that okay?"

"Okay, madam."

Biase watched them move out. She could not take her thoughts off the plight of Yamua, who had lost three children to sickle cell anaemia. She could not help wondering what the genotype of his two remaining children was. As far as she was concerned, Bunkar looked strong and sturdy and far from any health issues. Biase had to call for that break because she needed time alone to quickly think over and process all what had been discussed, before their next meeting.

Lunch time over, it was time for Bunkar, Sharma, their parents and Biase to come together again. Biase was now ready to do a final cross matching of all information received.

"I welcome you back. This is going to be a very short meeting, just a formality. I only want to categorically find out if your words march each other. We'll just spend about an hour doing that and I'll let you fathers go and bond more with your sons, take an evening stroll around the environment before it is dinner time. Then go for dinner together because I can see that this is one of the fundamentally missing occurrences in your homes."

All four men nodded and once again corroborated all information about them. When she popped the big question to the young men, "Why did you both engage in violence?" none of them could utter a word, their forlorn look going from their fathers to Biase, and then to each other. Biase was sure that they were genuinely sober.

"I say it again and won't get tired of saying it. Violence does no one any good. It is negative and destructive and you do not gain anything from it. See how your actions have dragged out your fathers for questioning. Consider the pain you must have caused your mothers. Does this make you proud of your actions? Do you know how much embarrassment you have caused everybody?" Biase charged at them.

The young men were faced down and silent. Biase looked on for some time. She decided forthwith to be gentlier with them.

"Gentlemen," she said. "I think we have had a long day and need some rest. Please let's meet again tomorrow morning. I would like to have another chat with you, the parents. Let's meet here by 9.00am tomorrow. We'll call in the young men when we are done. Good night all."

"Good night Madam." They responded and made for the door. But Biase who was slightly troubled, called back the two fathers.

"Sorry about the little change of mind I had. Take back your seats please, let's clear an issue." They were still trying to sit down when Biase began to ask her questions.

"Mr. Yamua, your earlier submission appeared to be incomplete. You told us that you lost three kids to sickle cell anaemia, and thereafter had two other children. Your story stirred my interest so much that I wondered what the status of the two children could be. You left me wondering." Yamua went blank and just moped. "Did you try to confirm their Rhesus Factor? Did you see a doctor?"

The man just moped.

"Mr. Yamua!" Biase jolted him.

"Yes madam, sorry I, I, I have something to tell you."

"Fine, go ahead, please," Biase said. Yamua looked at Tonzaka and Biase before opening up.

"I did not confirm anything. I did not see any doctor. The children simply made us forget the bitter past as we watched them grow under our roof. The important factor there is that they were healthy and did not die. They restored our joy and we love them hugely."

"Hmm! How wonderful! Good to know. But is that all you said you had to tell me?"

"Yes madam, for now."

"That's okay. Thanks for the information. I suggest that they go for a test later, just for knowledge sake."

"Thank you, madam. See you tomorrow." Yamua got up as if in a hurry to leave.

Alone once more, Biase's head was full and near confusion. She needed to unwind so she turned on the television and watched an entertainment channel. Soon, Room Service brought the dinner she had ordered. She ate slowly, watching the television and wondering how many more hurdles she had ahead. Her eyes soon felt heavy; she dragged a yawn and threw punches in the air to beat the threatening sleepiness.

"I got reports to tidy up. Sleep is the last item I want now on my agenda."

The threatening sleep conquered Biase as she dozed off on the couch, with the television still on.

# CHAPTER TWENTY-EIGHT

# Well Done, My Girl

Biase has had her eyes wide open after over two hours of sound sleep. She could not tell what woke her up but she shortly began to hear the voice of a worthy companion, as in a vision.

"Well done, my girl! You are doing quite a good job. But be sure to get a combination of satisfactory and shocking results. Just watch. Life sometimes is like that. Also note that all your sufferings of the past were for a purpose, to make you a well-rounded and fulfilled individual and to highlight your female resilient trait and power. Your life has indeed been a lesson: evil has no gain! And it is hoped that people will learn from it. Another lesson is this: If you find yourself in the valley of life's circumstances, do not remain in the valley, work yourself up to the mountain top of success. The waves of destiny toss people around and get them to meet unexpectedly with each other. It is all for a purpose, for a lesson. Never forget favours. You must not forget all those whose good deeds the waves of destiny brought your way. And because you are such a resourceful lady, the President will give you another task to carry out in the Niger Delta area – the riverine area that turned your life around. You see, your destiny cannot completely be severed from the Niger Delta. Congratulations, Biase."

Then there was a long pause. Now completely awake, Biase waited to hear more. But the voice had vanished.

"Thank you," She found herself whispering, "must be the Companion."

She sprang up and looked around. She tried to ruminate over the words, which she knew she heard loud and clear.

"Hmm! Everybody has a companion but not everybody has the privilege of discovering theirs. I promise to obey every instruction of the Companion. I'm all thanks." And heaving a sigh of relief, she added, "I really value this sort of classified information, instruction and counselling, specially delivered to me."

Sleep was now hard to find for Biase. The Companion's voice kept ringing in her heart. 'You must not forget all those whose good deeds the waves of destiny brought your way'.

She took her wrist watch from the table and peered into it, muttering, "2:00 am." Then she picked up her cell phone and selected a number and began to speak.

"I'm sorry, darling. Just have to disturb you now."

"Biase, are you okay? Anything the matter?" The baritone voice sounded surprised.

"Lande, I'm fine but I need your help. I'm so sorry I have to wake you up from sleep. Darling I am sorry, okay?

"It's okay. What's the matter? Why are you not sleeping?"

"I need us to get in touch once more with Community Network News (CNN), Female Rights Advancement Project (FRAP), Shores Clinic 2 and the Raboni Home."

"What about, this time and why so sudden?"

"I don't know oh. You may call it inspiration, conscience, trance or whatever, but it's a strong feeling, it's a prompting. I was roused from sleep by it. I must do it or I'll be restless."

"Okay, darling, we'll do it. Just try and go back to sleep. We'll fine-tune everything later today. Now, promise me you'll go back to sleep."

"I promise."

"Great! Goodnight, darling. Love you."

"Love you too. Goodnight."

"Hmm, Lande, what would I do without you?" she said to herself. Hours later that morning, they talked further and decided on what exactly to do, after Lande had tried to make some contacts.

"B, I could not find the contacts for most of those institutions. You know it's been a long time. I don't even know if some of those organisations still exist. I know that Raboni is still there but for one to get to Shores Clinic, one has to ferry across. As for Sophie, we have been talking."

"Oh thanks, Lande." Biase paused and said, "but we have to find a way to further acknowledge their efforts. It's been long since we last made contact with the organisations."

"Sweetheart, we could write a book to tell the world what happened. The book will serve as acknowledgement of the efforts of all those mentioned. You can do a book, yes you can, B. I am sure everything is still in your head so start jotting things down as usual. Is that okay, dear?

"Hmm, a book? Yes a book! I'll write a book to tell the world what happened; and appreciate the true heroes. The book will also create an avenue for all to note that evil doers will eventually meet with doom. In the tiny community of Pionto, a snake appeared from nowhere and gave a rapist a fatal bite, immediately after the inglorious act. The book will recommend death penalty for rapists, under any guise. It will also..."

"Hey baby girl, you still have not forgotten all that?" Biase hissed.

"Lande, will I ever forget that? Does anyone ever forget horror? Anyway, thanks for the suggestion, I'll write a book. By God's grace, I will."

"That's my girl!" Lande made a fist.

# CHAPTER TWENTY-NINE

# Calm an Enraged Lion

Biase sat waiting for Tonzaka and Yamua. She had earlier told their sons to wait for her call before joining them. She was pleasantly surprised when the dads, once more, walked into her hotel room together. Her hearty greeting betrayed her excitement.

"Good morning, gentlemen!"

"Good morning, madam!"

"Please sit. I don't need to ask, I know you had a good night's rest. I hope you had talks with your sons after the meeting of yesterday."

They both nodded more than once, each now with a pensive look.

"So how did it go? I'd really like you to increase the bonding between you and your children."

"We'll try," Yamua answered and Tonzaka said yes.

"Going back to our former discussions, would you blame peer pressure for your children's bad behaviour?"

"Peer pressure plays a major role but there are other factors hidden from the parents. So we might have limited knowledge," Yamua confessed.

Biase turned the swivel chair on which she sat, now facing Tonzaka, "Would you also blame it on peer pressure?" she asked.

"Honestly, I do not know. I think I am getting a bit confused."

"No need to get confused. Together, we are working on a project. So far, we are not doing badly. We shall soon get there, okay?"

"Okay, madam. This your voice can calm even an enraged lion. Thank you."

"Wow! Enraged lion? Thanks, Tonzaka. Let me ask you one question."

"One question?"

"Yes, one question. What is the meaning of Shamar in your language?"

"I am not sure there is any word like Shamar in my language"

"But it is your son's name or is it not his real name?"

"Nooh, Shamar is just a nick name. His real name is Ismail."

"I see," Biase muttered, planting a strong gaze on Shamar's father, urging him, with unspoken words, to go on.

"He is the only son we have, in fact the only child. I refused to marry other wives even though I am entitled to. Our consolation is that he is strong in our religion. He is quite strong willed too, but kind of stubborn."

"Was n't that quite risky? Your only son, only child for that matter; he could have been killed in any of the riots he spearheaded. What if any such thing had happened?" Biase intended to prick his heart.

"Thank God it did not happen like that oo. God be praised. Thank God you are here. This thing must stop."

"Yes, thank God. But for this to stop, parents have to be closer to their children and try to understand when and why their behaviour starts changing. This way a lot can be nipped in the bud." She paused and took a deep breath, looking into space, then jotted down something and began to speak again, looking at Tonzaka and Yamua.

"Fathers of riot group leaders!" Biase called out to them and both men shook their heads in rejection of that name.

"I am quite glad that the sworn enemies are now softening their stance, having been made to understand that cruelty is as evil as those who practise it. I can't place my finger on exactly why and how they got this far." She took another deep breath and looked at both of them and asked, "Now what do I make of this?" She turned to Yamua.

"I am cork sure that Bunkar is also a nick name. What is your son's real name?"

"He has many names..."

"Which one is he known by?" Biase's voice was slightly raised.

"Ah madam, wait small." His voiced quaked as he said those words.

Baise and Tonzaka looked at him expecting him to talk more. He sighed.

"Before that, let me say this." Yamua said. "When my children all died, we decided to put an end to our sorrow by fostering two kids at a time; a boy and a girl. We became very happy. People began to call my wife, mother of twin boy and girl."

"This is great information, Yamua, why were you hesitant? So one of the twins is Bunkar." Yamua nodded.

"And what is his real name?"

"His real name is Isaac. He had the name from the Home and we loved it."

"From the Home?"

"Yes, where we adopted him from."

"You adopted him from a Home? There are a few of such Homes in different locations. Can you remember the name of this Home?"

"Em, em, ah, em..." Yamua bit his finger, rolling his eyeballs. "I'll remember it, just give me some time. This thing happened over twenty years ago." He hissed.

"How old would Bunkar be now?" Biase asked, trying to follow.

"He should be about 23 years old?"

"That is the age for adolescence blues. As adolescents, they seem to be at war with themselves and their environment. They want to rebel against constituted laws and authority. Teenage and adolescence years are usually the toughest time for parents and guardians. Any slip gets them to drift and perhaps trip. If you ask me, I think it is the most active part of youth."

The silence that followed was deafening. It was as if no one knew what else to say. Biase was now thinking hard, aloud.

They were tensed up, all three, and quiet. They looked on, but Biase spoke again.

"Let's get the young men in."

Using the hotel Intercom, she instructed her aides to ask Bunkar and Shamar to come in.

# CHAPTER THIRTY

# Oh My God!

All five now together once more, Biase exchanged pleasantries with them and drew their attention to the table by the corner which had some biscuits, bottled water, fruit juice, bananas and groundnuts. Her first question in this segment was directed at Bunkar's father.

"Mr. Yamua, have you remembered the name of the Home?"

"Yes, yes, I have. I hope I am correct. It's a long time ago. I think they were calling it em, em…"

"There you go again. That means you have not remembered the name…"

"I have, I have. It's just that I am not too sure which one it is and it looks like I am getting confused. One happened in Kaduna but we had to travel far for the other. I don't know if the name has changed now but it was called, I think, the, the…

"The what? Mr. Yamua, talk to us!" Biase raised her voice again but calmed down soon after, on realising that she had been slightly impatient.

"Okay, Mr. Yamua, just take it easy and try to remember. We'll wait."

All eyes now fixed on Mr. Yamua, his discomfort was glaring.

"There is something like 'privilege' in the name. I am remembering now. Yes, Raboni Home for the Underprivileged. In the remote community of…"

"Oh! That's the name of the Home," shouted Shamar's father.

"What do you mean Mr. Tonzaka?" Biase asked as Bunkar and Shamar looked on, surprised and wondering what the adults were up to. Bunkar got up and went to his father and asked him what was actually going on? His father signalled him to keep calm. "I'll explain everything to you, please." He told his son, who slowly walked back to his seat. Tonzaka continued.

"I am sorry, madam. I did not know how to say it earlier and Mr. Yamua's sickle cell anaemia story weighed me down too so I could not talk. I became confused."

"Yes, Mr. Tonzaka. Please feel free to talk now, we are listening." Biase, slightly impatient, urged him, her heartbeat pacey. Shamar's father, after trying hard to avoid Biase's gaze and Shamar's eyes, made a startling confession, looking down and talking slowly. He was visibly upset.

"I am also not the biological father of Shamar."

"Dad! What are you saying? What does that mean? Biological… Whose are you?" Shamar cried out.

"Son, forgive me." He burst into a loud cry, and talking amid tears, he continued "Forgive me. I didn't mean to let you know, ever. There was no need, you are my son and nothing can change that."

Shamar could not raise his face. He did not want to look at the man who had just said he was not his biological father but who at the same time claimed that he was his son. But Tonzaka walked slowly up to him and rubbed his back, trying to say something. Shamar gave him a violent push, turned around and bent over, cupping his hands over his face. Tonzaka had hit his left hip on the ground as a result of the push and had fallen on his back. Yamua and Bunkar rushed to lift him. Dazed, he staggered but they held him and prevented him from falling again. Shamar raised his head again and everybody thanked God that the glare in his eyes was not a loaded rifle."

"Liar! Liar! Liar!" He howled, stamping his right foot on the floor.

Biase was so scared she had to put the security guards on the alert. Her heartbeat raced even faster. Tonzaka quivered. Yamua and Bunkar had an uneasy calm. It had not quite dawned on them what was really going on. They were just surprised.

"My son," Tonzaka managed to speak again. "It is the truth. I am not lying to you. Please believe me. We love you as much as any biological father can love his son. You are the only child we have. Your mother and I tried but could not have a baby, so we had to adopt you, a beautiful bouncing baby boy. Please forgive me, son. It was all beyond our control. We are happy we have you. Nothing can change it."

"Shamar, I will not have you insult your father in my presence. Nothing on earth gives you the right to call him a liar. What has come over you? Or have you gone crazy? What do you mean?" Biase gripped by anger and uncertainties, and hearing her own heart beat, scolded and jolted Shamar who sharply looked at her, confused and helpless. "You must tender an unreserved apology to Mr. Tonzaka before I can proceed." Shamar got up immediately, walked to his father and went down on both knees, clasping his father's legs in his arms and looking upward with teary eyes.

"Baba, I am very sorry, forgive me." Tears flowed freely from father and son.

"That's okay, my son. You have not offended me." He rubbed Shamar's head with both hands. "You have the right to get upset in this circumstance. Get up, my son. I am sorry for getting you this hurt. I know how strong the tie is. It can never be severed, not even at this point. Get up, son. You see, it was either your mother could not give me a child or I could not make her do so. We had to get you to console ourselves. We really love you." Tonzaka bent toward the kneeling young man and tried to lift him up. Shamar got up and they both got locked in a long hug.

"I'm sorry, ma. I'm sorry sir." He said to Biase and Yamua, shrugged and took his seat.

"That's my boy!" Biase was indeed pleased with Shamar and with herself. "Come here, give me a hug!" Shamar obeyed. She was glad that her hard work had not been in vain and that she had succeeded in softening hardened adolescent rioters.

"I think we should allow your dad to continue with what he was saying." They cast pensive and furtive looks at one another. Biase reached out to the table at the corner and poured out some water for herself, and went back to her seat. She felt her tummy churn.

"Please go over to the table and help yourselves, we need a little break."

That appeared to be a very welcome invitation. No one imagined how thirsty Shamar had been until they watched him gulp several glasses of water. He wiped off sweat from his forehead, face and neck. Bunkar went for a glass of fruit juice while Yamua and Tonzaka just watched, unable to eat anything. Yamua's heart was pounding. He was thinking of what to say to Bunkar. Biase noticed that tension had been doused somewhat, then she spoke again.

"Mr. Tonzaka, we are listening to you. Please continue," Biase urged.

Tonzaka grinned. "Eh heen. A close business associate and friend of mine helped me to adopt my son, Ismail, from a Home. I could not remember the name until Mr. Yamua mentioned names that sounded like it. I'm not sure but..."

Tonzaka went silent. Biase felt a serious bowel movement. She also felt like throwing up. She excused herself. Right in the convenience of the hotel, she found relief, and after sprinkling water from the sink tap on her face and wiping it with a towel, she stepped out to join the rest.

"I am sorry about that. I had a slight stomach upset. Go on, Mr. Tonzaka. You were really making sense.'

"Okay, thank you. Sorry, madam, about your stomach."

"Thanks, I am okay now." Everybody voiced their own 'sorry madam' and Tonzaka continued with his remarks.

"In fact, his name then was Ishmael but we had to rename him Ismail, which is the Muslim version of the same name." Biase could not take notes any longer. She was not even sure that she was still listening. She was shivering like she had a fever. Her stomach threatened again and she hurried once more into the toilet and sat for about eight minutes producing only watery substance while her tummy continued churning. Her whole face was covered with sweat. After about ten minutes, she slowly came out, apologetic. No one knew what was wrong with her but they sympathised.

Tonzaka continued. "Sorry, madam. I remember they told us that Ismail's twin brother was adopted just two hours before we got to the

Home. We felt depressed because we honestly would have adopted them both but thank God, we got Ismail, who from childhood had been strong in the religion."

"Stop! Stop!" Biase screamed as her body visibly shook. She stood up, sat down, walked about, sat down again and placed her head on the table. She actually fainted. They all watched her chest puff up and down. Then finding renewed strength after about ten minutes, she sprang up and began to scream again.

"Oh my God! Ooh! Ooh! O my God! Could this be them? Could this be true? What is happening to me oh? Heey! Is this my destiny? Could this be true? Oh my God! Oh my God! Hey! God oo! Help me oo!" Biase lamented, screaming even louder, truly tormented. She threw herself on the chair and laid her head on the table again, for a while, then raised her head once more, closed her eyes tightly and stood up. Her head whirled, her legs wobbled and she dropped into the three-seater sofa that was unoccupied and stretched herself, eyes tightly closed. She opened her eyes but could not see those sitting there and watching the drama incomprehensibly. Tears, only tears!

"Did we do anything wrong? Is she upset or sick? I hope she is a normal being. This is quite strange or was her drink poisoned?" Tonzaka whispered, wondering.

"Let's give her more time, it may be nothing actually. You know she is a woman. They have different moods. After some time, if the situation does not change, we could alert the hotel authorities," Yamua said. Shamar and Bunkar could not utter a word, their eyes were just wide open. They both had never witnessed this kind of action before. Eyes still closed, Biase raised her head slowly and sat up. She reclined and sent her head back, now facing the ceiling. She slowly opened her teary eyes and also very slowly, got up from her seat and paced slowly away from the outer part of the hotel suite which served as her workplace. She went to the inner room, sat on the bed, tried to lie down but sprang up quickly and went out to meet the rest. Her imagination went on a spree as her eyes explored the flabbergasted young men. She paced about the room as if in a trance. Everybody gazed at her, amazed. Biase's body was covered with sweat, in the air conditioned room.

"Madam, are you okay?" Tonzaka asked, truly worried. Yamua, lost in thought, could not talk. He only observed what was going on.

"Ma'am, daddy, please what is happening? I'm lost! What is it about this Home? What Home are you talking about?" asked Bunkar. Shamar had become like iced water.

Biase braced up, trying to conquer her emotions.

"Your home, my children, where you both were born," Biase said in a calculated manner.

"Your home, my children, where bla bla bla!" Bunkar mimicked. "What's all that?" Distraught, he turned to his father.

"Please, daddy, can you explain this better? What's going on here? It is killing me." Bunkar was in dire need of help.

"I am very sorry, my son, I should have told you the truth myself. But right now, to be frank, I do not quite understand the unfolding scenario."

"What unfolding scenario? Daddy, did you lie to me? Did you deceive me? And my sister?"

Yamua tried to go close to his son.

"Leave me alone!" Bunkar shouted and moved away from him to a corner where he could brood.

"God, what does all this mean?" queried Bunkar's father.

"I don't understand oh. How can she be their biological mother? She looks too young to be," wondered Shamar's father.

Biase was not listening to them. She was painfully dealing with serious internal issues. All of a sudden, she shouted, looking at the young men and hitting her chest with her right palm, "I am your mother!" She signalled the young men to stand up and they did. She held the two of them and did not let go until she had emptied 'pints' of tears on them. Then she slowly went back to her seat and gently sat down and started talking to them.

"Isaac, Ishmael! My sons! You are my twin sons! I had you when I was seventeen. Due to some cruel circumstances, I had you twin brothers in a Home. Please no more Bunkar and Shamar! I thank God for this day, the day I saw you again with my two eyes. I bless the day I found you, and thank God Almighty." She was looking upwards and crying again. "I will tell you how it all happened so you can free your minds and have nothing against your parents. You did not create yourselves, neither did you place yourselves in these two families. You first lived in my womb. This is where you resided for nine months," she said as she clutched her belly. "You see, you are brothers, twin brothers. And you were going to kill each other?" Ishmael and Isaac exchanged a look. "I want you to note that violence is evil and needless. You were not born evil, so please resist that society that wants to turn you evil. Be good citizens and take this life the way you have seen it. Nothing is in your hands. Can you imagine how you lived in my womb? What was your relationship in the womb? You were that close and now so far apart. Not any more, by God's grace. For your information, I have some other children from the same womb but your destiny lies in these parents here." She pointed at Tonzaka and Yamua. "Cherish and continue to love them. Later, another meeting, outside official work will be arranged. You will also get to meet your other siblings. Your parents will tell you when that will take place. Thank God you both have good parents who love you. That's my joy. May God protect and guide you and your parents!"

"Amen!" they responded.

Biase, breathing slowly but deeply, stopped talking and silence followed. It was as if everybody had gone dumb. Biase, slowly turning to her sons, Isaac and Ishmael, broke the silence.

"Now you agree that Bunkar and Shamar are dead forever and Isaac and Ishmael or Ismail, as the case may be, live on, and that henceforth, you'll be good citizens. No more riots. Do you promise?"

"We promise, Mother." Isaac affirmed.

Biase nearly fainted again.

"Yes, Mother, we promise," Ismail confirmed.

Biase, hearing them call her mother for the first time, shut her eyes tightly and sat hard on the chair, taking a deep breath. Her body quaked and her skin goose-bumped. Gripped by a fainting fit, she placed her head on the table again, on top of her folded arms. It took a while before she could raise her head. The young men who were confounded wondered what kind of magic, happenstance or miracle made it possible for their trainer, counsellor and mentor to also be their biological mother. All eyes were on her as she swallowed hard and slowly began to tell them the story of how the waves of destiny had tossed them all to the point where they were, at that moment. By the time she finished telling them the whole story of her life, laying emphasis on the boat mishap, the rape and pregnancy, streams of tears flowed freely and deep groans were heavily emitted. Biase made sure she informed them all that the man who made her pregnant had long died, his parents also. And that there was no need to ever imagine or think of seeing or knowing them, even for a moment.

"I have moved on, and want you to also move on. It is true what they say that once there is life, there is hope. Let's keep this hope alive! Live your lives with renewed hope. Refrain from evil, abhor rape, knowing that you are products of rape and that rape led you into this journey. Restrain yourselves!"

Isaac's father was sighted facing the wall at one corner of the room and actually leaning against the wall, wiping his eyes intermittently with his handkerchief, blowing his nose while Ismail's father found it convenient to sit on the floor and lament his life, amid tears and groans. Biase's handkerchief was so soaked it could be wrung. Ismail and Isaac now shivering, with big goosebumps all over their skins, and eyes as red as blood, spontaneously stood up, giving each other a strong unwavering look, their chests puffing up and down. Pacing towards each other, arms stretched out sideways, they quickly got locked in a tight and long embrace, with four eyeballs tightly shut, releasing streams of tears.

END

www.ingramcontent.com/pod-product-compliance
Lightning Source LLC
Chambersburg PA
CBHW062038120526
44592CB00035B/1263